THE NEW GIRLS

Drastic Choices.

I sincerely hope that my story
lets people facing the same or similar decisions
know they are not alone.

Copyright 2018
Janice Anne Wheeler

Cover design by Kimberly Smith
NE Print Solutions, Plattsburgh, New York
neprintsolutions.com

For all of you who made me what I am.
You know who you are.

TABLE OF CONTENTS

The New Girls
Drastic Choices

The New Girls

PRELUDE

On the afternoon of May 24, 2002 I was driving west on I-70 in Colorado. As I crested the hill above Georgetown my phone rang. On the line was my Mother's former oncologist. Former, because he did not save her life. Former, because she is gone and he is no longer on my list of employables. Former, because I was done with him. Former, as of yesterday. She had died yesterday. Yesterday.

He did not take time to empathize or offer small talk. Instead he was direct and to the point, an attribute I generally admire. There are a couple of studies, he ventured, that I would like you to be part of. The first, an experiment with tamoxifen, I turn down flat. No poisons for me, thanks. I had little use for Big Pharma then and not much more now.

The second study is a new genetic test, he explained. It could tell you of your risk. Not interested, I replied, with all the youth and anger of a thirty-something who lost her mother without even a month's notice. She was my best friend, my mentor, my teacher, my critic, my sounding board, my travel companion. I was a bit lost without her. Your risk is probably high, he persisted. I imagine so, I told him, hanging up the phone, but I do not want to know.

MARCH 7

It is just before 6am on a wintery Wednesday in 2018. The sun is barely rising over the Green Mountains of Vermont. The eerie grayish light is interesting enough to snap a photo. In spite of the butterflies in my stomach, I pause and capture the moment.

We walk into the third floor Surgical Waiting Room and tell the receptionist my name. They have the operating room reserved for a seven-and-a-half-hour block, she says, raising her eyebrows at me. I glance at my brother, my mouth already dry. I don't think we need that long, I replied.

We were here, in exactly this room, talking to exactly this receptionist, at exactly the same time, for another surgery, last August. Then it was a foreign world, outside our realm of experience, outside our realm of knowledge. Now we know more, but wish we did not.

The next hour is taken up with officials and consent forms and nurses and two surgeons and magic markers to ensure matching incisions and anesthesiologists and IV's and a gown that opens in the back. At 7:20 they wheel me into an incredibly bright, blue, intimidating, industrial room with at least a dozen masked, scrubbed experts ---straight out of a Hollywood movie. Their eyes are on me, wondering about today's work, wondering what brings me here. I feel my pulse go a little crazy, there are butterflies, lots of butterflies, in my stomach.

You cannot undo this, one of the Surgeons had told me, months ago. You have to be sure. With practiced ease they transfer me onto the operating table, introduce those eyes above the masks I had not yet met, and anesthetize me.

The next time I see a clock it is ten past five. The sunrise was barely peaking over the Green Mountains when I got here, and it is dark when I reawaken. My surgeons used every minute of the seven and a half hours.

I will never be the same.

8PM

The nurse requests that I stand up and walk, go to the bathroom. This seems insurmountable. I refer to myself as a strong girl often enough, yet I am challenged to the core by how I feel at this moment. Inch by inch I shift my legs and feet to the left side of the bed, experimentally, gingerly. As I attempt to stand and straighten, I do not feel strong. The nurse asks me the question I will become incredibly familiar with over the next two days; On a scale of one-to-ten with ten being the worst pain you can imagine; how would you rate your pain? Twenty-four, I promptly answered. Her smile was surprised, even a bit unbelieving. Not kidding, I breathed; my inhales only go down a third of the way. The rest of my torso will not straighten, my arms, when I move them even slightly, remind me how much damage has been done, how extensive the procedure is. I am on my own with the basic bodily functions, those things you take for granted in every day life. Incredible begins to describe it; far different than anything I have ever experienced.

10PM

What looks like a twelve-year-old in a white Doctor's coat appears at my bed side. To my drugged vision it was Doogie Howser. He tells me I should get up and walk. I tell him no. He tells me I should try to use the bathroom again. I tell him no. He asks me if I can lift my arms. I tell him no. He asks me if he can check my surgical site. I tell him that's probably his job and he hesitantly unsnaps the backless gown at the shoulders, exposing my chest. The incisions are beautiful, he tells me. I smile, just a little. They don't feel beautiful, I tell him.

I ask him for a drink of water. He is tall and awkward, surprised at my request, but tries his best. Perhaps they don't teach bendy straws in Med school. His intentions are golden.

The nurse comes in for my vital signs around mid-night and comments on the young Doctor. He always seems so nervous, she observes. I nod. His responsibilities seem huge to me; wandering a teaching hospital at night walking into rooms with no idea what to expect, what he will see, who he will meet, what they will say, what he will say. He sees people when they feel their worst, or are elated. Imagine the tremendous range of emotions in a hospital, from the pain and joy of childbirth to milestones such as mine to death and unanswerable questions. I briefly contemplate that many years of education; I could not have done it.

2AM

My pulse drops to forty-four, which sets off an alarm. They reprogram the monitoring machine to alarm at forty. My pulse drops to thirty-nine, which sets off the alarm. It is against regulation to turn it off. I do not sleep.

4AM

My entire torso is on fire. Not exaggerating the pain level, it feels damn close to top of the chart ten at all times. Bring on the oxy-whatever it is, I think, dependency be damned! It is the only thing that calms the intensity. I ring the nurse's station. She is wonderful and perceptive; she comes with painkillers in hand. No wonder all those folks are addicted to them, they allow you to feel nothing, which sometimes, only sometimes, is exactly what you need. For three hours I seem to float above the bed in a fog.

I sleep a little.   I cannot look down at myself, I cannot take that step.

MARCH 8

Not moving is best. Not moving is the only option I have. The trek to the bathroom is a marathon. Breakfast? No. My brother brings me coffee, holds the cup and straw. Moving my body is nearly impossible, and arms only to the elbows. Very quickly I learn that we use our pectoral muscles for nearly everything except walking. Brushing your teeth? Yes. Holding a book, a tablet, a phone? Yes. Wiping your ass? Yes. The no lifting for six weeks, restriction seems like it might be an easy enough request. No driving? OK we can do that with family close by. But here's the thing. After this kind of surgery, you cannot, cannot lift your arms above your shoulders without a crazy painful reminder. T-Rex Arms the plastic surgeon team says, a friend and I call them Seal Flippers. Keep the elbows glued to the ribcage. This is not an easy task.

The drains. There are four three-foot long tubes with little pouches to catch fluid from the surgical site—what??---These come out underneath my arms further complicating everything I used to do for myself without a second thought. They go home with me for the first week, two of them I keep for three long weeks.

The drains are a little creepy. Clear plastic tubing is arranged inside of me to come directly out of the skin on both sides of my upper chest, near where my breasts had been for, well, darn near as long as I can remember. These pouches become my nemesis, my constant companions and reminders of what path I chose.

My plastic surgery team consists of all beautiful people. Seriously beautiful people. So, if it's not bad enough when your beautiful lady surgeon sees the unnatural state of your body, when her pair of tall, dark and handsome interns examine it, that's probably even a bit worse. I wonder how I look and then laugh at myself. Not the time for that particular train of thought.

The incisions are perfect, he tells me, his companion agrees. She's the best, I reply, and I didn't want anything less than that. She is, he said, absolutely. Their genuine bedside manner is as good as they are attractive.

A nurse admires the interns, my roommate chuckles. Oh yes, there's a roommate. My procedure was elective. Hospitals remind you that most procedures are not, and how lucky I am to be able to choose my path. Her attitude is amazing in the face of pain and uncertainty, her family by her side. She tells my brother that I am beautiful, which I am not. She is a compassionate, suffering angel, and as I write this I wonder about her fate.

A minor reaction to a prescription keeps me another night, against my wishes. The handsome intern squats down by the side of my bed, bringing his eyes to my level. Are we negotiating? I inquire, not wanting to stay. No, he says. Sorry. The pulse alarms are the same, the ceiling is the same, the pain is the same.

Only I am not the same.

MARCH 9

I look at the passenger seat of my car and cannot imagine how I can sit in that position. For an hour. As with all the other tests along this path, of course I do, none of this is elective now. Rate your pain on a scale of one to ten, my brother jokes, the twentieth time I've heard this request in two days. I got this, I reply, laughing, but we are in the double digits here. He rises to the challenge of trying to figure out where to put the drains, how to loop the seatbelt around the back of the seat, how to get me home.

My backless gown is soft, blue pin-striped, long and comfortable. On impulse and to reduce the process of changing clothes, I wear it home. And I wear it for the next three weeks. I wear it and wear it. Best thing I have ever stolen. Now I know why they design those gowns as they do. They're not sexy, but they let you get to all the parts you need to get to.

We add a bit of red wine back into my evening routine. At least something feels normal.

LAST JULY

When your Doctor's office calls to schedule an appointment to discuss test results, those test results aren't negative. You don't need an appointment for good news. You need an appointment for difficult news, complicated news, 'bad' news; positive test results. Most of us have been there, and if you haven't, well, lucky you. These appointments generally lead to a lack of appetite, butterflies in the stomach, restless sleep, if any. These appointments lead to experiences none of us want and most of us never imagined. Let's hope, for all our sakes, they are few and far between.

I go to the appointment alone and when she enters I speak first. I don't need them, I tell her, frightened to the core, I don't need any of those parts. The test results indicate that I possess the BRCA2 Genetic Mutation. BRCA stands for Breast Cancer, and there are two different mutations, 1 and 2. Both indicate incredibly high risk of Breast and Ovarian Cancer, increased risk of Melanoma, Peritoneal, Pancreatic, the list goes on, all nearly equally frightening. The Breast Cancer risk is eighty-seven percent in my lifetime. Eighty-seven percent. It feels like a certainty. Like a death sentence. The decision to have surgery was nearly as quick as my gut reaction to the news.

I had picked up a copy of the twenty-page lab results a couple of days prior, done a little research. The report lay by the side of my bed for days, weeks maybe. Reinforcing my resolve. Reinforcing my logical, clinical decision to remove healthy organs from my currently healthy body.

Knowledge is Power. Knowledge can lead to prevention. Knowledge sometimes means you can outsmart what the statistics say is going to happen to you. Knowledge is a double edged sword. Do you always know what you should know?

I had been surprised to get that call from the Oncologist all those years ago. Western Medicine? I felt that if they knew anything my Mother would still be alive. She and I would be deciding where to have lunch. Her Wedding Invitations, already printed, would have been sent out that summer as scheduled. I don't want to die, she said to me from her hospital bed, my life is too good right now. You're not going to die, I had replied quickly, confidently, easily.

Her surgeon described her as 'salvageable' the day we pulled her from a life support system that her Proxy clearly told them she did not want. Clearly. She had, in fact, underlined the "No" artificial means of support, not once but three times. We all had copies of this. I still do; it is etched in my memory. It is hard to know what to keep and what to leave behind.

My mother turned sixty-three on May 1st, just past the five-year anniversary of her successful battle with Breast Cancer. Admitted to the hospital for surgery May 5th. New Primary Cancer, Peritoneal, diagnosis May 6. Gone May 23rd. Gone. Groceries still in the fridge. Car in the garage. Answering machine blinking. Towels on the rack. Dishes in the sink. Hummingbird feeder still half full. She was gone.

We got the official diagnoses at our appointment in the Oncologist's office, so you know it wasn't good news. Peritoneal, the nurse said. Never heard of it, I reply, bewildered. Spell it for me? I request, and she does, not able to look me in the eye. The lining of the abdomen, she explains, not too helpfully.

No one looked us in the eye that day. My mother is in pain, stunned, frightened at this new attack on her body. That day started this tiny little butterfly in my stomach that stayed with me for weeks, months even. For long after she was gone. It's the same little butterfly that appears when someone tells me about someone with Cancer. It's the same little butterfly I get when I think of losing another family member, or a friend, or an acquaintance to that damned disease. In fact, that butterfly flutters when I read about Cancer, or walk down the hallway in the hospital past the signs labeling treatment locations and offices where they try to beat it, to figure out where it comes from, to figure out why it occurs.

I used to get those butterflies when I read the plastic card in my shower reminding me about breast self-exams. So much impact on my life. I lost my best friend, my mother, in her prime. My Grandmother. My Aunt, my Uncle. My Great Aunt.

What doesn't kill you makes you stronger, one of my Mom's favorite wisdom bombs. What does kill you, well, kills you.

Now we believe, my mother was never tested, she endowed both my brother and I with is the BRCA2 mutation. I think it is the word itself that bothers my brother the most. Mutation, he says, focusing on the terminology; I don't like telling people I have a mutation. While I concur, at least he doesn't have to tell people he has undergone a Prophylactic Double Mastectomy with Reconstruction, which is the official term for what I have done.

MARCH 11

I am home in bed, flat on my back, with a heating pad and two Beagles. The nightstand looks like a drugstore. What are you doing, my friends inquire, texting frequently. I barely even reply. Surviving, I think to myself. I got up the stairs. When I wake it takes me a quarter of an hour to build up the fortitude to sit up in bed. Come on, strong girl, I cajole myself. Prove it. And eventually, each morning, I do. But I do not feel strong.

I cannot imagine the strength of people diagnosed with Breast Cancer who have to face treatments such as Chemotherapy and Radiation after this surgery. It is nearly inconceivable. Those women (and some men, my Uncle died of Breast Cancer) are strong; my hat is off to them, my respect goes deeper than I can even describe. I want to know more of them, hang out with them, gain knowledge and compassion and perception. I lost my Mother before she was able to pass on all that wisdom.

I'm coming over to wash your hair, a friend tells me. No, I respond. Not up for it. The hours pass in a fog. I think I can quit the Oxycodone but I cannot relax, cannot sleep. A two-time Breast Cancer survivor and confidant reprimands me for trying to go without it. It relaxes you and lets you heal, she tells me. You need to be able to rest. Be comfortable.

I am not good at doing nothing, yet that is exactly what I do. It's the only thing that works.

I'm writing a book; I tell my stepmother. Good, she replies. My only dilemma today is that I cannot type on a keypad, it's too far forward to reach. This book forms in my brain and wants badly to get out into black and white.

The enormity of what I have done sinks in. I still do not look at the work they did. It does not feel like me.

MARCH 12

When I awaken this morning it takes me a mere ten minutes to gather my strength to rise. That's much better than the fifteen minutes it took me all last week....

I express to my friend from Georgia, who checks in every day, that I am going a bit mad. Should I come up there? he asks. Nothing you can do, I say. Nothing anyone can do. One of our soldiers is down! he describes me to me, his voice confused, concerned and wonderful to hear.

The confusion, I think, comes from the reality that I chose this. Of my own free will, I signed the papers and decided to remove healthy organs from my body. As a preventative. Opted to have a procedure that would cause me discomfort for months, as it turns out. There is comfort, however, in the knowledge that I did the right thing; I remain steadfast in that belief.

MARCH 14

Seven days after the operation I can breathe almost half way into my lungs, elbows absolutely still stuck to my ribcage. The drains are, as we've discussed, weird. Four plastic tubes stick out from somewhere deep inside my chest. It is simply not natural, a little grotesque. My surgical teams seem so used to all of this they think nothing of it. If it is not something you have seen, it can make the fine hairs on the back of your neck do a little dance if not stand completely straight up. Not natural.

Making it even more unnatural is the fluid that constantly accumulates in them. What is that stuff? I ask my brother rhetorically, how can it just keep coming out of me? He is diligent, gentle, taking care of me, his little sister. He empties the drains, replaces the bandages, and measures. Not natural.

I DON'T KNOW EXACTLY WHAT DAY

I have an extreme moment of self-pity. I don't know if I would have done this had I known the pain, I confide in my brother. The incapacity. The lack of ability to take care of myself. The pain.

He raises his eyebrows in surprise, he is silent. I rarely show weakness even when it occurs. Who doesn't have moments of regret, hindsight? We all do, and more often than we wish to. I remember sighing and going back to bed.

That afternoon I brace myself, get up, brush my teeth and do FaceTime with my dad, in the nursing home. My self-pity vanishes. Vanishes. I made a choice to change my life. His life is permanently changed, for the worse, by a disease and no choice of his own. He cannot take care of himself, he cannot communicate clearly, he cannot leave the building, cannot leave the wheelchair on his own.

As I sign off my selfishness is overwhelming and I cry. I cry those big, expressive sobs that come when you are sad that you are less of a person than you thought you were. It is such a disappointment to be someone other than what you believed. The beauty in that disappointment is that you can change it, you can learn from it. What a lesson I got that day.

MARCH 15

My follow-up appointments with the surgeons are this afternoon and tomorrow morning. Eight days after my surgery, I have not looked, but think I have prepared myself. I know I made the right choice, I know I am one of the lucky ones, to have chosen this route instead of having it thrust upon me.

While the pain is less, it remains like a constant pressure on my ribcage, and when I move my arms it becomes more distinctive, more acute and radiates further, around and under, sometimes all the way to where the muscles meet my spine. It does not feel like me.

It does not look like me, either. I knew I would never be the same when I awoke in the hospital. When I lay eyes on the results of the surgery it is a shock, but in all honesty not as disturbing as I had anticipated. I study myself in the mirror, take a strong, deep breath, tuck in my tummy and move on with my day.

My friend arrives to help me into my clothes and jacket, take me to Vermont. We have one life to live, and we can only go forward, not back, not sideways. Forward.

You never know exactly when you will catch the ferry so you have to have a little leeway on this particular North Country commute. We are grabbing a glass of wine with thirty minutes to spare before my appointment; don't judge, this is how we roll. I am wearing a borrowed zip-up hoodie and have a body that is not familiar to me. My chest is concave, the four drains are tucked in the front pockets, bulging unexpectedly, unattractively, at my waist. I am used to being attractive, to catching people's eye. Not that I am beautiful in a classic sense, but I have a presence, a style that sets me apart.

There are a dozen patrons in the pub, and I need to use the ladies room. So I take the only route there is, a rather long walk past all the other customers. Upon my return, my friend tells me: You're very real. It is one of the most solid compliments I have ever received and I will never forget it.

They're perfect, the Breast Surgeon tells me after a brief inspection of her work. Perfect. See you in a year. Her role is over. The breast tissue is removed to the best of her ability, and her reputation proceeds her; she has years of research and a crazy amount of surgeries under her belt.

What will they look like? I had asked. They look deflated, the surgeon told me, shrugging slightly. She has seen hundreds. As of this morning I have seen two. Her description is accurate; they do look deflated, indented where my B-size used to protrude. All the skin remains and so is gathered, like a curtain, across either side. The nipples are farther apart than I remembered, swept to the outside by the lack of flesh beneath them. Remarkably, there is no bruising, no discoloration. My brother and I say, over and over, how is that possible? For seven-and-a-half hours they cut, scraped, poked, prodded, removed, inserted expanders and stitched. How can I not have any bruising? Amazing.

I ask her how she accomplished that. Most people have at least a little, she tells me, shrugging again. She knows the body is a mystery, as much as she wants to know all the intricacies, no two are ever the same. The nipple-sparing procedure is a pain in the ass, she had told me at our pre-op appointment. I'll do it for you, she responds to my amazed expression, holding up both hands against my protests, but it's a pain in the ass. She is known for her candor, her feistiness. I am glad she is mine.

The Surgeon is reaching for the doorknob as I express my thanks as well as compliment her skills. You've been talking to my mother, she quips, and is gone down the hall to the next patient, her next case. She is efficient, caring and dishearteningly busy dealing with Breast Cancer and all that it entails. She doesn't save all her patients, she cannot. I walk out of her office healthy, a success in her book, but not everyone does. Folks in the waiting rooms at the Breast Center are all shapes, ages and sizes. Cancer is not prejudicial; it is frighteningly common.

You know what I say again? How lucky I am to have the choice.

Due to the distance, an overnight in Burlington works great to catch both today's and tomorrow's follow-up appointments. We have a tremendous asset and are able to check into the American Cancer Society's (ACS) Hope Lodge. This place is peaceful, solid, quiet, friendly, and a little sad, a fortress against whatever may happen next door at the hospital. A night spent at the Hope Lodge readjusts your perspective, triggers your compassion. It teaches you that there are people, people from all walks of life, suffering far worse egregiousness than you probably ever will. Children on chemotherapy, adults fighting the disease without companionship. Their demeanor is generally upbeat, their attitudes to be admired and mirrored.

The Burlington Hope Lodge is a regal old brick home redone by the ACS to house people fighting cancer or cancer related processes. Everyone is welcome, long term, short term, whatever is necessary. You see families forever bound together by the fight that they did not choose, that was thrust upon them. That fight is a common bond.

There are always snacks in the kitchen along with complimentary breakfast and dinner. I have created donated dinners for the twenty or so guests and it is one of the most rewarding things I have ever done, giving back. The people utilizing The Hope Lodge provide even more assurance of how lucky I am. I was able to plan this procedure, make it happen when I wanted to. The women who operate it are special, calm, intuitive, rule-abiding citizens complete with a therapy dog.

One of the rules is no alcohol, and unfortunately we cannot abide with that, sneaking bottle and opaque plastic glasses in with our luggage. We uncork a red wine when we arrive, a daily ritual for my Friend Basket, wherever we may be. It is normal, it is routine, in a world where currently most things are not.

MARCH 16

I am half-awake, half dressed, sipping coffee. A voice from our bathroom interrupts my wandering thoughts. I can't believe you're going to be fifty, she tells me. Her comment takes me by surprise; it is launched from left field, early in the morning, out of the blue. I laugh. Right?! I reply. The laughter requires an inhale and I do so cautiously, my torso tender; breathing all the way in still a challenge. I continue to laugh. If it wasn't for the twelve inches of fine stitches across my ribcage I would not be able to stop laughing.

It does not seem possible to me, either. How could I be turning fifty this year?! So many big events happened in 1968 that there are constant reminders with 50th anniversary celebrations, and on and on. Fifty, Fifty, Fifty. We talk about how old fifty used to seem, and how now it's easy to say something happened thirty years ago and feel like our parents. Her vocalization stays with me, but is no longer an important thing. It is a state of mind, of how we feel and how we approach things.

There is a sign in my brother's kitchen, it's my kitchen, now, too, that asks, How old would you be if you didn't know how old you are? Love that expression, that question. Age is a state of mind, an attitude, a direction. I have gotten to the point where I see people my age and think, geez, I can't look that old! Perception is reality, so I'm going with that. I laugh again, it IS the best medicine, and remind my commentator that she is not that many years behind me...

At this morning's post-op visit, the plastic surgery team removes two of the four drains from underneath my arms. The removal process is a highly unusual sensation and one I hesitate to even describe. Breathe in, the physician's assistant requests. She pulls an impossibly long piece of tubing out of my body, Band-Aids the tiny incisions, and half the drains are gone. They also start the expansion process, which is a great surprise and feels like progress. It turns out to be a different sort of pressure, but completely tolerable.

During the Reconstruction portion of the original surgery expanders are placed underneath the pectoral muscles on top of the rib cage to eventually recreate the space that my new breasts will be placed in; not under the skin but under the muscle. How's that for a weird concept for those of us (me!) who know nothing of plastic surgery and breast implants. There is a port on the top of the expanders that a needle slips easily into. Another thing I never wanted to learn, my brother and I say, laughing. The learning curve continues; they expand me one hundred milliliters of saline on each side which effectively levels out the indentations left by removing all the breast tissue. It is progress, indeed!

I do, however, go back to not seeing myself, as it still looks nothing like me. Cover up your mirrors, my plastic surgeon had advised during our original consult. I choose to simply avert my eyes.

MARCH 17

Two years ago on St. Patrick's Day a girlfriend and I spent the night in Key West Florida. Had a little trouble finding the B&B after dancing, drinking and celebrating with the locals, as I recall. Way too much fun to be had in that town! Enjoy every minute, that's our motto. Makes great stories, great memories, great friendships.

This year the Irish Holiday is my first day up and about, showered on my own and feeling a little bit human. First day back to visit my dad in the Nursing Home. Pushing a wheelchair? No. Driving? No. Still cannot hold a book, type on a keyboard. Drying my hair is a challenge; I end up kneeling on the floor, bent over like child's pose in Yoga, drying the back. I think I promised not to tell anyone that, but it's a laughable visual so I thought I would include it here. Being honest, aren't we?! Everything I do is at least a little awkward! Remember I still have six feet of clear plastic tubing hanging out of my body! Yikes. If you cannot laugh...

My elbows remain glued to my sides; reaching for a coffee mug in the morning takes my breath away. I have learned to leave things at waist level. The laundry detergent above the washer is insurmountable and I need to ask for help. It is a humbling experience, to say the very very least. And here I thought I was a pillar, able to do just fine with no one. The empathy I feel for my father continues to grow. He faces his inabilities with a smile and resolve.

My family has the hundredth conversation this year on how great it is that I am here, in the North Country, rather than somewhere else, so they can take care of me. And take care of me they do.

MARCH 20

The two remaining drains are slightly less cumbersome than all four and nearly full each morning. Where does all that come from? I again ask my brother as he performs his morning nurse duties. Seems like too much. He nods, measuring carefully and 'stripping' the lines so no clots form. Up to eight ounces of lymphatic fluid drains every twenty-four hours as my body heals itself. They stay in for twenty-two days. More than a gallon and a half. Seems like too much, I think. This may be at the top of the list of things I never wanted to know.

The drains are uncomfortable, dangling around me as a constant reminder of the choice I made, but they simply become the new normal. Selecting a wardrobe that has a spot to contain them is a challenge. My man-size baggy shirts come in handy. Remember I cannot raise my arms above my head, so it has to open in the front and be really soft, too! I opt for brushed tank tops as a comforting layer against the changes in my torso, the changes in my body, the psychology of feeling so different than I used to. Simply walking around the house and outside when Mother Nature allows helps me pass the time and become used to how I feel. I walk miles and miles.

LAST WINTER

Every evening my Stepmother and I check the time for tomorrow. Every morning we walk two blocks from our rental house to Atlantic Beach, South Carolina, to the ocean, to catch the sunrise.   Most days, they are stunning, no two are ever the same. Dark red to all shades of aqua, orange, blue, and purple. Watching the glowing sun crest the horizon is something that I have never tired of; I have thousands of photographs of it on this very Macintosh.   Even on cloudy days it is dramatic with crashing waves, shorebirds and many, many shades of gray.

The gulls and sandpipers hunt at the edge of the surf, playfully chasing the edges of the waves and the hapless creatures hiding there.   Our gentle German Shepherd Husky mix studies the world with his light blue eyes, understanding that these walks are our escape, our routine; they bring us joy, they bring us closer.

The tide leaves behind reflecting pools and an occasional treasure; a random, beautiful whole shell among the millions of tiny pieces crushed by decades of waves. We collect them and will forever have a little sand in our jacket pockets as a poignant reminder of these great walks.

When we return to the house we show the perfect shells to my father, who turns them over in his hand and gently places them on the side table, not wanting to know what we experience without him, yet treasuring them just as much as we do. Often, a sigh escapes him and he turns his blue eyes to the window, ending the interaction, showing his frustration, but only barely, and, as always, with grace.

This is our second winter together in North Myrtle Beach. My father is unable to join us for these sunrises. Diagnosed nearly two years ago with Progressive Supranuclear Palsy (PSP), the same man that climbed mountains in Western Colorado three years ago can no longer manage walks on the beach. The decline is heartbreaking. He accepts it with grace and laughter. His bright blue eyes belay his sadness but not often. Quiet strength is exuded when we talk about the disease. There is no treatment, there is no cure. There is just making the most of the time we have. When we contemplate the future and enjoy our final days my stepmother sums up how we feel, the mixed emotions as we head north. We may never pass this way again, she says. Her own wisdom bomb. Enjoy life while you can, take nothing for granted.

A year later we are in the Conference Room at the Nursing Home and I am at a loss for words in a meeting with the Administration. He is our Treasure, I tell them, tears welling up behind my eyes, and needs to be treated as such.

MARCH 23

When it becomes routine to dump your lymphatic fluid out of the drains, clean the tubes and measure it while your coffee brews, you know your life and your perspectives will forever be changed by this process, this journey.

During this afternoon's appointment, my plastic surgeon glances at me and my careful tracking of fluid removed from myself. The drains stay, she says decisively. It's usually three weeks, it has only been two. I'm sure I sighed.

On the upside we do another 'fill' of the expanders, and my breasts get just a little more shape, become a little more recognizable. The expansions push the muscle wall outward, causing a tightness that I still have trouble describing, particularly along the incision line. Duct tape perhaps? Or it may feel like those whalebone corsets the ladies used to wear to create a waist far smaller than it actually was. Maybe a girdle?

MARCH 26

I cannot hold the hardcover that is our Book Club book of the month. I do not watch television. I stare at the ceiling, listen to some music. Friends check in with me every day. How are you? they inquire. Feeling better? No, I tell them, not really better, maybe a little. What are you doing? they ask.

I am doing nothing. This lesson in patience is priceless, important. When we have no choice but to risk further damage and more pain, we are patient, waiting for resilience. I practice mindfulness, *The Power of Now* thinking and it makes a difference. There is only now, so make the best of it. The mind is a powerful force, a powerful tool.

Typing on a keyboard is incredibly challenging. In spite of the discomfort I start this book while things are fresh in my mind, fresh in my body. I go through several titles; *Knowledge is Power, Saving My Life, What to Leave Behind*, and finally settled on *The New Girls* because that's what I call them. And they are the protagonists.

MARCH 27

There is another effect of this surgery that is important; healing one step at a time allows me to gradually contemplate this topic, get my mind around the reality. The delicate process of removing breast tissue results in the removal, also, of your nerve endings, your feeling. Another foreign concept, another curve. So if I wasn't looking and you placed your hand on me, I would feel a bit of a pressure sensation but nothing on the skin. Thus far. This varies from person to person. They told me this, they warned me. My specific nipple-sparing procedure has the best results in terms of perhaps having some feeling return in the future. At this point I have a little sensation where the port is located and twinges are a regular happening, a nurse tells me those could, indeed, be nerves waking up. No guarantees. Not in this life.

Sometimes it's best not to dwell on things. I knew it was part of the deal, part of the downside. Probably the worst downside, actually, for me. I am single, searching for the right partner, looking at men my age and thinking they are too old for me, knowing I am not ready to feel old. The lack of sensation is a trade-off that I made for the security of knowing that I would keep these new parts forever.

I am now only a dozen years younger than my mother was when she died. That used to sound like a long time, but now it does not.

MARCH 30

The drains come out!!! Big breath in, the Physician's Assistant tells me after clipping the one suture that has held the drain under my arm for over three weeks. She pulls it cleanly out, that unique, hard to describe sensation, like none other I have felt before or since.

From my awkward angle it looks much longer than it could possibly be, several inches of clear plastic tucked neatly near the center of my chest while it was open on the operating table. Not natural. But now, gone! Progress, for certain.

Another expansion. Uncomfortable, and a continuing reminder that we are going forward.

APRIL FOOL'S DAY, ONE YEAR AGO

As my father's disease progresses, more and more often I contemplate destiny. What if we could control it, just a little? In the news Angelina Jolie has gone public with her prophylactic mastectomy. She chose this in response to her genetic predisposition to Breast Cancer, in her case BRCA1. At the time this seemed drastic to me; my perspective on that has certainly changed as I follow in her footsteps.

She and I removed not internal organs but external, exposed, symbols of womanhood and femininity and reproduction and sexuality. It is a drastic measure, a drastic choice, to be certain. But if you could prevent your own suffering, or lessen the chance of it by eighty-five percent, would you wager those odds? In Las Vegas if you had a hand that was eighty-seven percent, which was my risk of getting Breast Cancer, you would play that card. In the case of us with the risk, it is the opposite, eliminate the risk, eliminate the potential. If you have ever seen anyone suffer with or die from cancer, you know you would not wish that on anyone.

APRIL 5

My plastic surgeon is a rock star. I have known this since I saw her at a conference last October and we first met that November. She is smart, true, honest, talented, caring and meticulous. We have become friends. A procedure that she takes three and a half hours to complete other doctors reportedly do in less than two.

Today is my third expansion, one hundred milliliters per side. My brother , Nurse John, has driven me this time and for the full lesson has joined us in the procedure room. The expansion process is a bit Frankenstinian—modifying parts of your body after removing originals that were whole and happy and painless. These new parts have felt incredible pressure since the day they were installed. Today multiply that pressure a few times.

Yesterday John and I looked under my right arm, which has become a bit uncomfortable. There is a swollen area there, soft and fluidy. My surgeon examines it, with a small level of uncertainty, and a distinct attitude of forced nonchalance. Let's send you down to the Breast Center, Radiology, and just have them take a look, she says rhetorically, conversationally, decisively. Whatever you think is best, I reply, as always. I cook for a living, and do not need input on what we should do about this. I am here because these folks are the best and know what to do, how to do it and will get it done.

It is late afternoon, almost Happy Hour, and the University Breast Center cannot accommodate me until tomorrow. We head home, and are very pleased to note on the ferry that we had purchased a screw-top bottle of wine at our favorite store. Not that we don't have a corkscrew in the car, be assured, but those screw-tops make the job easier.

We toast on the ferry to countless things we have seen and we have learned this year that we never wanted to know. We laugh at the red wine in our insulated coffee mugs, we worry about the complication, we cry a bit, we hope it's not serious.

On the way home John drops me at the Nursing Home where our father has resided for nearly six months now. I spend a couple of hours a day here, sometimes more than that. I try to bring him snacks and dinner and smiles and stories and make his life better. Nursing homes are waiting rooms for the dying, waiting rooms for death. This sounds harsh and while I understand the place for them in our society, the need for them, I have pacts with my entire Friend Basket that I will never be placed in one, no matter what.

He smiles when he sees me. Big smile, bright blue eyes. Janice Anne! he beams. What an amazing feeling. I would not trade this time for anything.

APRIL 6

The very next day we return to Burlington--our commute to the Hospital takes us back across magnificent Lake Champlain. This north-south lake is headwaters to the mighty Hudson River, but is not particularly well known outside of the region. It is a monster and reportedly has a Monster, similar to Loch Ness. The largest freshwater in the US after the Great Lakes, Champlain is beautiful, one hundred and eighteen miles long, four hundred feet deep with islands, rugged shorelines, granite cliffs, and sandy beaches. On the east side Vermont's Green Mountains loom, the Western side displays the High Peaks of the Adirondacks, the oldest range in North America. On a clear day you can pick out the Lake Placid Winter Olympic Mountain, Whiteface.

Our standard commute; a fourteen-minute ferry ride from Plattsburgh to the Champlain Islands in Vermont, then we are treated to a scenic drive along the highway across narrow bridges with Osprey nests, State Parks, 50's era motels and apple orchards. A winery is just to our south; grape varieties must be chosen to withstand the thirty below temperatures that frequent the long winters here. They have been successful; vineyards, dairy operations and farms dot the landscape. Quintessential New England.

Marinas full of sail boats line both shores all the way to the Canadian border; summer is short and coveted here; locals soak up the sun like the rare commodity it is. As children we take nature's beauty for granted. The knowledge that life can change or be taken away on short notice make you appreciate so much more.

It is a rare day that I sit in my car during the ferry crossing, a rare day that I do not get out, take pictures, walk the stairs to the second story and admire Mother Nature's work. Today is a rare day. On this morning's ride back to Vermont, the wind has kicked up six foot waves that rock the boat and trigger my propensity for motion sickness. Unable to sleep last night, I am not in the mood for this latest indignity. The expanders feel a bit like a mule standing on my chest, or maybe a boa constrictor constricting. Hard to describe, hard to breathe, the butterflies awaken.

As I lay on the small surgical table contemplating that I have complications and it's a big deal and I'm freaking out I still do not question the tactic of removing these organs from my body. I surprise myself, under this morning's array of emotions, that still I do not question my decision.

It is not surprising that other people would make a judgment, show surprise, show doubt, but generally they do not. This does not mean that they would do the same in my position, it means that they support my decision from the practical standpoint.

Never judge someone until you walk in their shoes; another of my mother's wisdom bombs that I so badly wish I was still hearing. Don't assume you know how someone feels, or guess what you would have done, had you been them.

An older, conservative business partner looks right into my eyes and tells me, it's a no-brainer. I smile at him but do not even try to explain how much more complicated it is than that. Logically, practically, statistically, he is correct. From a purely logical standpoint, the preventative surgery is an easy choice, I am way ahead of the curve. Dropping your cancer risk from eighty-seven percent to two is a no-brainer indeed. Remember that the curve is one of those blind ones on an unfamiliar road so you slow down, even more than you might have needed to, because the unknown can be a damn frightening thing. I bring myself back to the present. Hopefully I have rounded all the curves.

Today's procedure is serious but at the same time simple, with a sonogram directing the needles to two little pools of fluid that have formed around the surgical site. I have never been able to watch needles entering my skin so I study a print on the wall. My PA and her assistant are careful, quiet, serious.

They have never seen expanders inside of someone, they tell me, intrigued. I thought this was quite interesting; my turn to be surprised. I supposed in a Breast Cancer clinic it would be quite common.

We did a little show and tell and I hoped I contributed something to their knowledge of the process, explaining what it felt like, the downsides and the realities. You can see the expander edges on the sonogram and it gave the three of us a point of reference, something of a connection. Their curiosity and lack of experience, encourage me even more to tell my story, to spread the word about BRCA and my experiences, no matter how personal, no matter how humbling.

The University of Vermont Breast Center proves its worth and the worth of its employees to me once again. Through this whole process I always felt the quality and the caring of the care. It has been a comfort, and I think it always will be. I sincerely hope they embrace this book and share my story with people facing these difficult decisions.

APRIL 7

My father turns eighty today, and he looks slightly unbelieving. When his father turned ninety we told him how old he was he retorted, Bullshit, I can't be that old; I'm quoting here, he lived to be a hundred, and couldn't believe that, either. He dismissed us out of hand, and looked away. Now isn't that an interesting situation? How old would you be if you didn't know how old you are?

One month from surgery I am feeling up to bringing dinner to the nursing home, reengaging my love of food and cooking. They let us move in to 'The Grand Room' which is not quite Grand but pretty darn nice and a great reprieve from my father's room and the constant chatter of televisions and nurse's aids as they go about their responsibilities.

The evenings there are quiet, the administration and sales staff is at home in their comfortable surroundings. We rearrange the furniture, break the rules and sneak in a bottle of wine for us to enjoy; can you see a pattern here?! A rare sip from our glasses makes dad feel as though he is one of us, because of course he is. It's just that our lives are so different than they used to be. This Birthday celebration, although joyous, has a twinge of sadness. Communication is hard, his smile is irresistible and always makes the situation as good as it can be.

My nephew joins us and brings younger energy, another generation that can not yet understand what being fifty or seventy or eighty can possibly feel like. Lucky him. We laugh. We are together.

My stepmother unveils the big birthday present; a large metal wall-hanging of a sun for his room. *You are my Sunshine, my only Sunshine...* That's their song and has been for as long as I can remember—you know the words. Everyone does. Turns out that all the entertainers that come to the Nursing Home for an hour or two a couple of times a month, well, they know it too, and sing their rendition of it often. We hesitate just a little bit, I swallow hard, when it comes to the last line. *Please don't take my Sunshine away....*

APRIL 13, A FRIDAY

Hmmm, the PA says. Did you see this? The doctor saw it last week, I reply. It was a tiny bump and clearly did not belong there. I had covered it with a Band-Aid as it was getting a little bit red. Between the surgery and now, an interior stitch had turned under the skin so that one of the ends is protruding slightly and causing a bump. Hmmm? They are cautious, they are never appear overtly concerned. They are professionals.

My rock star is in surgery when they consult with her via phone. Quick in-house surgical procedure is required; we'll get this fixed. The PA, my favorite, looks me in the eye. OK? She inquires. I'm sorry, she says, and she means it. Bright Lights, blue gowns, iodine. The other surgeon, who I had not met prior to this, shows me the culprit after he clips it off. Looks like a piece of fishing line, he says. To me, it is another incision, another scar, another reminder. Like all the other work they do, it is efficient and the seam closes quickly. One stitch, this one on the outside.

What kind of bra are you wearing? inquires one of the nurses. They don't want anything putting pressure or abrading the incisions yet. Not wearing one, that was the deal, I reply, smiling at her. Never again! Woo-hoo! I laugh. One of the upsides, that's for certain. Victoria's Secret Bras run over fifty dollars now, I tell her, and shopping for them, not my favorite.

The Surgeon promised these will never sag! We laugh.

APRIL 16

I wake up today closer to my old self. I can move, stretch, carry, pick things up without too much pain. The tightening in my chest is so much less! I can breathe all the way in, I can take strides, I can reach the laundry detergent. Washing my hair is not a character building exercise. Wiping my ass is not such a challenge that you have to hold your breath to get through it.

After the surgery until now, I sat sideways on the toilet because it is situated, as most bathrooms are, with the toilet paper to one side, and you did not want to reach in that direction after this surgery, let me tell you! When I found myself in this position, the toilet paper roll right in front of me, it made my life just a tiny bit better. It was a small step forward, a victory! It was one of those things you never thought of before, and perhaps hope to never need again. And it made me laugh. Oh, we must always laugh.

Such a relief, such a difference from the nearly forty days and nights of not being able to do anything particularly helpful, or useful, or fun, or interesting. Of not doing much of anything at all. My brother remains steadfast in his care and concern. Above and beyond, for certain.

TWO YEARS AGO

'Everything happens for a reason' is bullshit, because, really? This phrase is a copout. It allows you to not take responsibility for what you could have modified. Of course, sometimes you are unable to modify your situation. And I get that. But sometimes, maybe even often, you could have. The acceptance of bad results that were within your control, that you could have made better, is a copout, everything happens for a reason.

If there is a reason for everything, presumably a good reason, how could my mother die at one of the happiest times she had ever known? Finally, the life of her dreams, a man who worshipped the ground she walked on, a beautiful summer home in Colorado, a house on a golf course in the Carolinas. He welcomed her and us into his life with big, long, open arms. What reason could there possibly be to take her from us? A friend of mine told me, after she passed, God needed her more than you did. No, I said, decisively. Not possible.

If there is a reason for everything, how could my father be suffering such a difficult end to his life? He was caring, thoughtful, smart and driven. A wonderful teacher and role model, his short bouts of temper taught me patience and acceptance just as his long bouts of patience and attention to detail made me who I am today. Why should a good man suffer when criminals are healthy and happy? It is circumstances such as this that make me question the wisdom of this common phrase.

In a way, I admire people who believe in something enough, their version of God, of a Greater Power, to not question what happens, to accept it with quiet grace and dignity. They believe that their loved one is in a better place, that it happened for a reason. Call me selfish. I wanted my mother to live. She wanted to live.

My mother was happy. Happiness is easy when you are young. Ice cream and rock bass and wild strawberries and corn on the cob; these things all make you genuinely, thoroughly happy. It's simpler. As we age we tend to need more to get that happy. Why is that? We forget that sunshine is one of the best feelings in the world because someone told us that sun is bad for you, dangerous, causes life threatening diseases and on and on. We forget that a simple walk outdoors soothes the soul and the nerves and clears the air of our days. An apple pie or macaroni and cheese bring comfort. Holding someone's hand, watching the sunrise. Life is better when you let the simple things make you happy.

After my mother died, I flew to North Carolina to pack her belongings and finalize a few things. On the first leg of my flight I sat next to a gentleman who had experienced my pain just a year prior. He helped me like few others were able to with his gentle wisdom and perspective. At the airport we drank Bloody Mary's and toasted our Moms and he left me in the executive lounge in Charlotte while he went to meet his fiancé'.

I was young and surprised that a connection such as that could happen; he had helped me through a difficult time. Such connections have been modifying my life ever since. Flying home from Colorado a few years ago a blue suited businessman, no tie, had the aisle seat. I am always a window girl; have to see what's out there, what we are passing by, over, and near. The sky and the earth are amazing to me.

We exchanged hellos as he sat down, nothing out of the ordinary. I had been fully prepared to delve into the latest historical fiction best seller, and pulled it out of my bag. Your ring, he stated. It tells me you are a free spirit, an entrepreneur, you think out of the box. I wear a ring on the pointer finger of my left hand with a unique design and tiny stones, and had for a dozen years or so: long before it was trendy. He continued to tell me about myself, and was disconcertingly accurate, astonishingly intuitive. You are adrift, he declared, you are undecided. I laughed, a little uncomfortable, a little amazed.

My life at that time was certainly in transition. He was a motivational speaker and absolutely correct. I will never forget our conversation; we talked for three hours. I confided many things in him. I was worried because I had not yet chosen the right partner to share my life, worried that perhaps I expected too much. Don't go down an ordinary path, he advised, it will not work for you, it will disappoint you. My path has been many things, few of them ordinary.

APRIL 20

Minor complication, we got this, one more of those little stitches; it's rare, a quick little in-office fix. OK. It's a journey. I got this. My skin is thin, they tell me. Perhaps in reality, I think, but as the expression goes my skin is definitely not thin.

On the way far upside, today is the final fill! They maximize the capacity of the expanders. Ouch! That is a crazy feeling! Now I know exactly where they are placed. Protruding slightly out under each arm, more so than the original girls, they are rock-solid, yes, rock-solid, and awkward. Before they had been unobtrusive, somewhere in there, now they are obvious, bulky, rigid. I think they are noticeable, but of course they are not. I have already gotten used to not wearing a bra. Why would I? These babies aren't going anywhere, and the rock star promised that they are never going to sag...

Through this process I think less and less about what people think. My brother, of course, is my constant companion in all of this. He has taken his role so much in stride I love him even more, which I did not think was possible. Your husband? people inquire. My brother, I respond each time. Most people are surprised, some respectful, some curious.

Our relationship is unusual and I realize it more and more. We come first with each other, should push come to shove, and it has. We have been apart for months at a time and when we reunite it's like it was before, through spouses and tragedies and cancer and holidays and adventures. He's had my back since I was able to walk and when I went to live on the other side of the country, he still had my back. And I have his. We are a team right now especially; after eighteen months living in the same house, we finish each other's sentences, we worry about our father, we make red wine, we drink Crown Royal.

When our mother was diagnosed the second time I picked him up at the Denver airport; he had with him the largest duffle bag ever made! I had no idea how long you needed me, he said. I told my boss I would let him know when I would be back, they can fire me if they want to. He stayed for the duration, of course, sleeping in her room when I needed him to and had my back.

THREE YEARS AGO

I am on a beach in the Bahamas. Sitting with my back to the bright sunshine, I gaze out onto water that is impossibly dozens of shades of turquoise and blue and darker blue. Watching the occasional whitecaps far out in the Atlantic, I ponder my situation. I know what I need to do, I tell my companion, I need to move on. Yes, she replies.

Seven months later I drove away from Colorado, my home for more than two decades. My house and business sold, a few possessions tucked into a storage unit, what I needed tucked into my trunk.

When I look back at that part of my time here on earth I miss it; I refer to it as my ex-life. It's hard to know what to keep and what to leave behind.

Leaving was the right thing to do; it led me back to my family with the time to take care of them and for them to take care of me when we all needed it the most. The pieces fell into place.

Perhaps that time, it did happen for a reason.

APRIL 30

My standard weekly checkup. Or not, sigh. Same minor complication, in two places, this time in my other breast. It's rare, quick little in-office fix they tell me again. Two tiny incisions, two tiny stitches on the outside. This is a slightly bumpier journey than I want it to be, but my path is clear, my confidence in my doctors and my decision are as rock-solid as these expanders.

I see and study the four small incisions on my previously unmarked skin. Geez, that skin has rarely even seen the sun much less a scalpel! I have a few scars on my body, and do not mind them. They tell stories of experiences, adventures and mistakes.

My worst scar is from a head-on car accident in Australia; it took forty-seven stiches to pull the back of my left arm together, some on the inside, some on the outside. While that scar bothered me for a while, I do not ever see it and the impact has long ago faded.

After three hours of sewing up my arm, the Emergency Room Doctor in Tasmania calmly explained to me that there was no skin left on my forehead to sew. We would have to hope for the best, she told me, and I'm quoting here. I am sure I paled when given that particular piece of information. Special tape covered my forehead, all of it, for weeks. A new invention at the time, you simply waited for the skin to regrow underneath the bandages and trimmed them off little by little. As I traveled on the other side of the planet we trimmed those bandages and we pulled the stiches out as they healed. Scars. What doesn't kill you makes you stronger.

That week of vacation was tinged with homesickness but the humanity and generosity of the Australians will never be forgotten. The meteorologist who pulled us out of the crushed vehicle took us into his home for an entire week! We slept in his daughter's bed, ate his food and drank his tea.

As soon as possible, I wrapped my broken ribs and went exploring. Our rescuer, who was a meteorologist with incredible knowledge, showed us the mythological creatures of Tasmania—wombats, devils and platypus. What an incredible experience. I got to pet the belly of a Tasmanian Devil! Those wild rides in his Land Rover further reinforced my desire to live, travel, meet people, breathe deeply. Appreciate the little things.

When my mother first saw my scarred left arm after the accident she pursed her lips, disapproving. Well that's not pretty, is it, she asked rhetorically. I laughed. No, it's definitely not pretty. She never shirked her words, always told the truth. I miss her every day. Sometimes the scars are on the surface and sometimes they are not.

As I write this I wonder why the twelve or so inches of scar on my chest do not bother me. They are long, but small and light, and perhaps most importantly hidden from the everyday casual glance. I have been given silicone tape to lessen their appearance but use it only minimally. You cannot see them unless my arms are above my head or you are kneeling at my feet, an interesting visual! And, more importantly I'm sure, *I* cannot see them when I look in the mirror or down at my chest.

Now, months later, I see myself with clarity and acceptance. Perhaps they have become badges of honor marking my journey, marking the defeat of the odds.

I fly to a business conference with the two tiny exterior stitches protruding through my new silk shirts. I hesitate to go through the metal detectors because I have been warned that the expander ports can set them off. In fact, each expander comes with a little ID card that I carry with me, explaining what foreign parts are in my body. I do not want this to happen; I do not want to have to explain this to a stranger, I am not ready. The metal detector fails to register my unique parts. I am relieved although I could also see a bit of humor in having such a conversation with, say, one of the nineteen-year-old male TSA agents that predominate my local airport.

The conference gives me a chance to see and ask my only confidant in attendance the question that is constantly on my mind; If you didn't know, you wouldn't know, would you? Probably improper English but none-the-less I wonder this constantly. To me they are so different, they feel so different. To the casual observer, not different at all.

MAY 1

I hate May.

It's that simple.

My Mom's birthday, Mother's Day, her untimely death. Three weeks of sleeping in a hospital room on a lounge chair, never imagining what was next.

MAY 11

Back to the plastic surgeon, the unexpected exterior stiches are all out, the skin is smooth and creamy, with barely pink tiny lines, my relief is palpable. The journey continues. We combine appointments to save us a ferry ride and do pre-op for the next step. The final step. June eighteenth--removal of the expanders and insertion of permanent silicone implants. The New Girls.

She is talking quickly as the territory is familiar to her. Liposuction? I repeat, stunned. My plastic surgeon nods. But you're not fat enough, she says. Perhaps this is one of the reasons I adore her. We may have to go inner thigh, or flanks. What? I ask. This part is new to me, completely new. Not only did I never expect to have a plastic surgeon, I absolutely never expected to have liposuction! Mental note: I need to Google Liposuction, as it is so far off my radar I never imagined it would happen to me.

Liposuction is used to fill the edges around the permanent implants with my own tissue. The process; insert a little tube and suck out my fat, pop it into a centrifuge to extract excess liquid, then put it where they want it. How's THAT for unnatural, my brain is screaming. Really? I ask unintelligently, forehead furrowing. I trust your judgment completely, I tell her, as I sign the consent. But wow that makes me uncomfortable and it not something I want to do, frankly. One of these days I 'll do some research and make a final decision. Of course, I do not contradict her, the decision has been made. She is my rock star surgeon and may have more diplomas on the wall than I have ever seen.

Minutes later we are sitting in the scheduling office and she tells me offhandedly that I'll need to wear Spanx. Like Sphinx? I respond. What is that? Never heard of those. How do you spell that? Spoken like a true skinny person, she laughs. They are clothes that make you look a little thinner, like compression. (Like whale bone corsets, I think to myself). You'll wear them for six weeks after liposuction. Really? I ask again, redundantly. Not interested! But breaking the rules after all these months is not an option either.

The inventor of this compression clothing is one of the wealthiest women in the country, my surgeon tells me. Americans love to feel thin, this much is true. She laughs at my lack of knowledge of cosmetic surgery, cosmetic clothing, fancy shoes. I laugh with her. I am wearing my brown Caterpillar boots (yes the heavy equipment company); they are well worn and I love them. I bought them in black last fall. I don't do fancy clothes. My brown V-neck cotton sweater was purchased from Cabela's (yes the hunting equipment company), my jeans are American Eagle, slightly baggy and comfortable with a sort-of matching studded leather belt. One of my favorite winter outfits, it suits me. Spanx? Not so much.

I am an outdoor enthusiast, incredibly conscious about my body, always have been, always feel like I could stand to lose a little weight. I have never considered myself skinny; at one hundred-thirty-five pounds I carry myself well but am rock solid, not skinny. If I want to look better I eat celery for a few days, extra time lunging or on the elliptical. I rarely eat all or exactly what I want. No sugar, super low carbs, honey in my coffee. Nutrition nut. Had no idea there was a clothing line that offered a much easier option! LOL, Spanx. Now I am required to buy some.

I admit to having an affinity for fancy underwear. Perhaps it's the contradiction between that and the Caterpillar boots, the hiking gear, the plain cotton tank tops and cut-offs that are my summer standard. It's better to keep some things a mystery, of that I am sure. Spanx should remain a mystery. I have no interest.

MAY 13

Wearing crampons to be safe, I climb my favorite fire tower, Poke-O-Moonshine Mountain, for the first time since February.

It is such a relief to be doing something so normal that I tear up at the top, taking the usual shadow-shots, proving to myself and the world that I was there.

Lucky to be alive, lucky to be able to do whatever I wish.

MAY 15

I was sitting at a bar perhaps five weeks ago and hear an unfamiliar voice call my name, I look up. A stranger calls out her maiden name, pointing to herself. Holy Shit!-- I cannot help but say—we were on the swim team in high school together. What are you doing here? What are you doing here? she laughs in reply. I live here! So do I! I blurt out. As I depart that evening I walk over to her table to say goodbye and meet the husband. I have showered with your wife, I tell him, leaning over. So have I, he replies, quickly. I like him.

She was my hero, that much is certain. We went to high school together in Central New York, ahem, thirty-three years ago, were on the swim team. My mentor still has records on the record board, was inducted into the Hall of Fame. She graduated a year ahead of me, we parted ways for decades, I had imagined forever. My High School is another place I simply never went back to, although the memories are good.

So with busy schedules and lives, it takes us weeks to find this date and sit face to face again with the girl I revered. Not just an amazing swimmer, a true, caring, smart, humble person with great parents and a great smile. Always supportive, always encouraging. After all these years we have an hour, which turns out to not be enough time.

We are at a sushi restaurant with the best rolls and the worst atmosphere you can imagine. Love that place for it's food and value and authenticity. Take it or leave it, is their attitude. This is what we are. They never seem to recognize me no matter how many times I go. It's an odd approach to customer service, indeed.

You go first, I tell her. We talk schools and jobs and a couple of mutual friends. You can summarize life in ten minutes if you skip some of the drama. Her story is cool; educated and re-educated, we both ended up with Cornell degrees, her dad is still living where we graduated high school. She went back to Ithaca and lived very near where I spent two long winters. She and her husband lived and worked blocks from each other for four years and never met. They were introduced and wondered how that was even possible. My favorite part of her story. How many times do we pass someone on the street that could mean the world to us but it never happens?

She is a five-year Breast Cancer survivor, just passed her anniversary. Double mastectomy, reconstruction. Her breast surgeon is my breast surgeon. Her plastic surgeon came from the same office as mine. I told them I didn't need those parts, she tells me. Now doesn't that sound familiar?

I tell my story, starting out at high school graduation and explaining how fate or destiny or both or neither brought me to Plattsburgh, New York, when I needed to be here the most. For the hundredth time (hundred and first time?) I shake my head at the timing of our lives; how people come and go and stay and pass through quickly.

I tell her what I have done, her eyebrows fly up. I wish I had known, she says emotionally. Me too, I say. I had no one to relate to. So often when you need that person, they appear. She offers her candid advice on mastectomies and recovery and offers any assistance that she is capable of. We hug, hard. One hour was definitely not enough.

My friend lost her Mom two years ago, I lost mine sixteen, we both tear up, it's impossible not to; we talk of the reality that it does not get any easier. In fact, the list of things I wish I could talk to her about just continues to grow.

I do talk to my Mom, it's just not the same. I would give up everything I have, everything, for one more day with my mother. Everything. One more day. That's my wish. You know what my mother would say to that? It doesn't matter what you wish for.

Her expressions and wisdom bombs were the best, they continue to ring true in everything I do. My favorite; when you travel, pack half as many clothes and twice as much money as you originally thought you needed. This one is spot-on and makes me laugh every time I share it, and I share it every chance I get. My mother was always right.

MAY 22

Spring green is my favorite color, my stepmom shares with me. I have known this for years, and it is worth repeating. Today, her birthday, she spends hours with my father, as she does every day. I have become even more convinced she is an angel and know that theirs is a great love story.

Every spring is a new beginning. New beginning is redundant, now that I think about it, but the intonation is so positive that nobody cares. Every day is a new beginning and that is a damn good thing. Some days just suck, no matter how optimistic a person you may be, no matter how full the glass. It is good to know that tomorrow we can start over, and not simply continue.

With a bit of warmth in the air and my father failing as we knew he would, there is a distinct feeling as time moves forward. The feeling is that we need to treasure every day, make the most of every moment. My father's diagnosis and prognosis are slowly becoming a reality. PSP takes the body and the mind simultaneously. Difficult to watch, it is far harder to imagine what the experience feels like to an intelligent, vital, active man. This disease, similar to the cancers on my maternal side, is potentially hereditary. In his case: no treatment, no cure. We want to believe that we know more than we do. The body and the mind are still a mystery.

My own mortality comes into focus. While this may be a selfish response, it is also a very human one, we relate our experiences back to ourselves. Events in our lives make us who we are; hopefully we can learn from them and adapt and be better the next time.

One of my favorite expressions; Say what needs to be said and do what needs to be done. In the years since leaving Colorado, I have taken this to heart. We hear every day of tragedy and loss and heartache. I would like to never again be caught wishing I had done something differently, left something important unsaid.

TWENTY-TWO YEARS AGO

Memorial Day Weekend— (the official start of summer!) my brother drove my Mom and her worldly possessions from Upstate New York to Summit County, Colorado. 1730 miles. When they end their journey Monday afternoon it is cold and snowing and downright wintery. It is the start of summer everywhere else. Her apartment in Frisco is close to 10,000 feet in elevation with views of three mountain ranges and Dillon Reservoir. It is quintessential Colorado, the cover of AAA or a tourist brochure. My mom had lived her entire life in New York; her friends are fairly convinced she has lost her mind. Retired from teaching and without a partner she takes the incredibly brave step of moving two thirds of the way across the country. She is ready for a new adventure, a new place, a new chapter; a new beginning; she knows only myself. We turn up the heat and pour Crown Royal. And we laugh. We are together.

I am surprised and thrilled that my Mother would follow me to Colorado. She and I have lived in different time zones since I was seventeen, on and off. We are very close; geography didn't matter; the actual date of the holiday didn't matter. We celebrated Christmas and New Years and Birthdays whenever we could be at the same table, drinking from the same bottle, breaking bread. The love of those family celebrations now seems as inherited as my BRCA2.

Petite and smiling and determined, she joins water aerobics at the local Rec Center, works for me at Copper Mountain, makes immediate friends. Eleven months later her Mammogram shows little white dots; they look like stars in a planetarium, shining through the dark breast tissue. If you are in a consult room and those dots are visible on the mammogram screen in front of you, someone's life is about to change. Forever.

They are not always cancer, we are told, and there is a new method, a better method, for testing these anomalies. Stereotactic biopsy is done by inserting a hollow needle near or through the suspect spot and drawing out tissue for evaluation. This test leaves the breast bruised and tender, as you imagine it would. When the diagnosis is cancer it leaves your spirit and your optimism a little bruised and battered as well.

Three days after the biopsy you are instructed to call and receive your news. In this case, on a payphone, for a quarter, in a parking lot in Denver where we were meeting friends. There is no scheduling an appointment due to the urgency of the news. The payphone was out of sight and earshot; she did not tell me where she was going. As clear as yesterday I can see her coming back around the corner of the brick building, arms outstretched to me. We didn't make it, babe, she said, her face crumpling.

The medical community was telling us we were lucky. They thought hers was a fairly good scenario. As if there is a good scenario. My opinion remains that there is not. Any person on the receiving end of the mammogram with the little white specs I can assure you does not feel lucky. That person does not feel that their scenario is particularly good.

She was always an incredibly positive person. Our glass is half full, literally; more than once she and I grabbed a margarita at the Mexican joint closest to her Oncologist prior to the appointments. Our glass is half full, figuratively; we caught the cancer early, it is non-invasive. The tumor is small. The consensus, the treatment plan, was lumpectomy with no follow-up, no radiation, no chemo. A simple elimination of the offending cells.

Our stumbling block came when the surgeon did not get a 'clean border' (oh, the cancer terms I know but never wanted to). A clean border means substantial cancer-free tissue around the tumor so there is no risk of contaminating or leaving behind anything that could then spread. She handles this distressing news with grace, she had been so happy not to be losing an entire breast.

The morning of the mastectomy she poses for pictures of the part to be amputated, removed in order to save her own life. I am the photographer at her request, it is an experience I will never forget. At the time I did not understand the magnitude of that moment; I had no idea how she felt. Or how it would flash back to me two decades later when I asked a friend to do the same thing for me. Like me two decades later, she never imagined herself using the phrase 'my plastic surgeon.'   But not exactly like me, her path was thrust upon her.

Two summers prior her sister had died, in her late fifties, after a very hard struggle with Breast Cancer that over time metastasized to the bone and brain. Long before mastectomy was the household word it is today, my aunt had both her breasts removed. It put her cancer in remission for quite some time, only to have it return with a vengeance. Her struggle was long and painful.

My cousins tested for BRCA and were found to not possess the mutation. Of the six in our generation, my brother and I are the sole carriers.

After my mother's first ominous diagnosis, we started to examine family history. On the maternal side, my great aunt died of Breast Cancer before we had the chance to know her, my grandmother Pearl fought valiantly against a Squamous Melanoma tumor that would not shrink or go away. She lost that battle in 1999. My uncle was found to have Breast Cancer in April of 2002; he succumbed over a decade later at his home on the Maine coast. Within days of his diagnosis, my mom discovered her second primary, unrelated as far as we know, to her first battle. Officially it was this, Peritoneal Cancer, that quickly took her life.

This family history is enough so that, every year before my mammogram when I recited the list, I got an eyebrow raise and genuine sympathy, empathy, concern, as there is such a connection with risk and history. Last fall when I had my final mammogram, which seemed unnecessary to me, the nurse, as usual, asked me if there were any changes.

Having been pre-op tested beyond my patience, I could not resist. My relatives are all dead, I replied, there are no changes. My brother? BRCA2 positive. She glanced away from her computer screen and raised her eyebrows even further. Just telling it like it is, my shrug said to her. It sucks.

It is important to note that only six percent of Breast Cancer patients are BRCA positive. Eighty-seven percent of BRCA positive patients end up with some form of Breast Cancer. Therefore, Breast Cancer does not indicate BRCA mutations, but the opposite majority is true.

There is an incredible amount of research on Cancer; an overwhelming amount, in fact. At times I feel as though one can find a study to reinforce whatever you wish to believe. Some will tell you meat is not healthy; some will tell you animal protein is what the body needs to fight disease. There are discussions on nutrition, exercise, body Ph, diet, heredity and many other topics. The fact remains that we know very little; each person is different and no single rule applies to everyone. I tend toward moderation, in my diet, in my life, in my beliefs.

On days when I am discouraged with the incredibly expensive machine that is our medical system in this country I also believe the conspiracy theories that indicate Cancer will never be cured because it employs too many people, is too lucrative. It would be immoral if this were true, and I hope that it is not.

LAST AUGUST

I received the BRCA2 results one week before I met with my Gynecological Oncologist (GYN ONC). Tall, fit and solemn, he looks at my chart, there is no small talk. As I anticipated we would, we discuss preventive hysterectomy, the official term: salpingo-oophorectomy. A perfunctory exam makes sure I am a healthy specimen; we discuss family history.

The next inquiry, casually made as if he was talking about the weather, takes me by surprise. What are you doing next Thursday, he asks, looking at a calendar on the wall. These six words more than any others have stayed imprinted in my brain. His sense of urgency, his carefully casual, matter-of-fact manner told me while I had other options, he recommended none of them. Let's get this done, and quickly, he was telling me. Because of the BRCA2 I would be scheduled for surgery at 6am next Thursday and would have a complete hysterectomy.

Other options? I ask anyway, a little intimidated, a little surprised. Not really, he replies. Ovaries, fallopian tubes, uterus, cervix. My hormone producers would be gone. So would my periods! That's the good news! Woo-hoo to that! Years of painful cycles, all over in one fell swoop. My glass half full, I'm all in. A definite upside.

Eight days later my brother and I check into that Third Floor Surgical waiting room for the first time, stay at the Hope Lodge for the first time. My soul mate flies in from Colorado, she and my brother bond over local microbrews.

I stay overnight in the Hospital with glue closing the tiny incisions on my hip bones (one for the camera and one for the tools; so interesting) and you can not see the tiny slit in my belly button. Nice neat little package. I am not allowed to vacuum or take out the trash, which does not break my heart. That procedure really was very easy for me, but you know now that is not the end of the story; few things are ever that simple.

Surgically Induced Menopause, excuse me, is that a thing?! Right, Surgically Induced Menopause. And for me, it was immediate. I had already started night sweats occasionally perhaps a year ago and could not imagine anything worse that that. Well, there are worse things than that. Hot flash on a date? Hot flash on an elevator? How about a little weight gain and slowed metabolism thrown in on the side of these annoyances? Growing old is not for sissies.

Help me! I said to my GYN ONC team. Help me now! Forty-eight hours into no ovaries my body is NOT happy! The PA is wonderful, caring, sympathetic. As soon as they allow me on hormone replacement therapy she says Congratulations! And she means it. Congratulations that I can cease the feeling that my youth is over. I'm dating, I tell her laughing, I cannot have these issues! I'm not ready!! She laughs with me, a dozen years older but sparkling with vitality. I know, she empathizes, I know.

The dates are few and far between anyway, I confide with a smile.

THIRTY YEARS AGO

It was a rare, bright, warm spring day in Upstate New York. Where the hell is Montana?!? My friends asked, stunned. What they meant is, what the hell are you doing? What the hell are you thinking? They are confounded.

The six of us transferred in from around the country and are Juniors at Cornell University's Hotel School; lounging between classes among the offspring of Marriotts and Hiltons. We call ourselves 'The Transfers.' None of us exactly fits in. The Ivy League school is small, eclectic, particular, expensive, accepts just a few of many applicants, and powerful. Influential, international. The best, so they say. So we say. Cornell Hotel is renowned world-wide; if you get this far, where we sit today, you are golden. You take the road of internships with the big Corporations, you follow the routine, you build your resume' with all the right employers. You get hired by the best in the business; probably also a Cornell Alumni, or a friend of one. Your advisor can get you where you want to be; the professors are as well connected as the students are blue-blood. It is a culture that you join, that you buy into, a club, an organization, a recruiting machine, as powerful a force in the industry then as it is now. If you do it right, and you work hard, it can take you to the top of your game. Beyond your imagination, perhaps. Every twenty-year olds' dream. Rich, a little famous, a little powerful. I do not fit the mold. My friends know this. My professors know this. My advisor knows this. I left and never went back. An oddity.

Our conversation makes me waver, but only for an instant. I should stay on the East Coast, take one of the offers. I do not. I interviewed with Disney, I interviewed with the best of them. They didn't feel right. I do not fit this mold. I am middle-class. I work three jobs to pay my way through Cornell, even with help from my parents and a student loan. I sleep on a futon on the floor in a room that is always too cold or too warm. My roommate and I bring home containers of food from our restaurant jobs to get us through our days off. My classmates come to the bar where I work and are surprised to see me working. They do not need to; their bills are paid. Their car is rust-free, their apartments well insulated, from both the weather and the real world. I am not like them.

On a whim between classes a few weeks ago I was flipping through summer job opportunities in the placement office. Filed neatly under "G", probably a couple of years before, (maybe even a few years before) is a simple, inexpensive tri-fold brochure about Glacier National Park and its concessions. Montana. The pictures catch my attention. Immediately. Never been there! So beautiful! Simply Glacier, it is called by those lucky enough to have set eyes on it. Look at the brochure! I tell them. I'm going.

At that time Glacier National Park concessions were contracted with Greyhound-Dial Corporation (yes, the bus, yes, the soap), and not surprisingly were looking for hospitality experts in all positions, for all the facilities in the Park. I call, on a land line, and they send me a two-page application, which I snail-mail back to them. I apply for a bartender position, that is what I want. It's what I do best, now, and I know the money will be good. They call, on a land line. The gentleman, with a faded British accent, offers me a job. But not the bartender job, the Restaurant Manager job. The Restaurant with two hundred and sixty seats. Serving three meals a day. With fifty-two employees. That job.

The offer: I work six days a week for two hundred and seventy-five dollars minus room and board. I made that much bartending just a couple of nights; I do not care. Clearly, they see me as an expert in hospitality, with a couple of years at Cornell and a whole resume of low-paying jobs with big adjectives. I am thrilled, honored, excited, ready for a road trip, ready for my next adventure. I'll be back for my Senior year.

I do the research, look through my Road Atlas, and start to plan. My mother was a great traveler; lucky us, we saw many parts of the country but even she had not ventured to the far reaches of Northwestern Montana. The chorus from my friends remained...they love me; they think I have lost my mind. I do not fit the mold. They love me because of this, they still think I am crazy. Perhaps they are right.

Many Glacier Hotel was completed in 1915, built by the Great Northern Railroad in an absolutely spectacular location. Spectacular. Nothing less than amazing. The hotel sits on Swiftcurrent Lake, has views to Grinnell Glacier, and you can cruise up the next lake, Josephine. When we went skinny-dipping on Josephine we would have to duck and hide to avoid the tourists on the boat. The scenery will forever be etched in my mind; the bear tracks on the trail I walked for exercise, the baby goats climbing sheer rock faces, the flowers, wow, the wildflowers. We walked up steep narrow trails to ancient waterfalls, enjoyed the sounds and sights of Mother Nature. Glacier has soul.

I am ignorant, of course, as to what this job truly entails. There are two hundred and forty rooms at Many Glacier, which is on the East side of Glacier-Waterton International Peace Park at the end of a dead-end road. It averages one hundred percent occupancy all summer long. Sold out. Tour groups, buses, families, hippies, international types, we get them all. On average we serve eight hundred meals a day. A day. Every day. My restaurant is the only place to eat except for the snack bar, which closes around six. They serve luke warm hot dogs and lots of soda. Every evening, with me at the hostess stand, there is a one to one-and-a-half hour wait to eat in the Ptarmigan Dining Room; we do not take reservations. This stuns our guests and makes my job as challenging as you can imagine. Most folks cannot pronounce Ptarmigan; they have not hiked the Park; they have not gotten off their bus. Most folks don't care about the indigenous wildlife, they're just hungry.

We watch bears every day, grizzly and black both. The sun shines every day. My room faces the lake, top floor. My room had the best view in the whole building. Imagine my New York self, driving a Mazda RX-7, living the dream in Montana. The hours were crazy, at least ten hours a day six days a week; I do not care. On the seventh day we got up early and hiked the mountains; miles and miles of pristine wilderness. When possible we combine two days off, the assistant manager covered the extra shifts, we went to Canada and explored Jasper and Banff and Lake Louise and experienced what the tour brochures tell you that you will. Go there! This is where I fell in love with the West.

My paychecks, after deductions, were $214 and change for sixty plus hours a week. That was the beginning of my Hospitality Career that continues to this day. You either love that business or you hate it.

NOVEMBER 4, 2017

We are boarding a direct flight from Orlando, Florida to Plattsburgh. Never heard of it? You are not alone. Plattsburgh sits in the very northeastern corner of Upstate New York. The North Country, as it is known, lies less than thirty miles from the Canadian border, with the Adirondack Park to the West, Lake Champlain to the East, creating the border between New York and Vermont. There is an amazing amount of Revolutionary and War of 1812 Battles fought here; many of the folks you read about in American History class have passed this way, most stayed for a time. Lots of ships, cargo and infantry both, rest quietly on the bottom of the Lake. Plattsburgh is one of the places on the planet I never thought I would live. The winters are long, cold and intense with a mere eight hours of sunlight at solstice, the weather changes quickly, generally not for the better, or so it seems.

I admittedly enjoy the summer and love the fall more than anywhere else I have experienced. September and October here are exquisite; filled with long, crisp, colorful, dry afternoons with heavenly dark blue skies. Warm days accompany nights that are cool; summer draws to an end with the most incredible hues in the hardwoods. I never tire of it.

Seeing the world is a passion of mine; I am a seasoned traveler, often by myself. I cannot get enough of the exploration, new places, smells, flavors, tastes, colors, views, people. Odd to admit, then, that only sometimes do I strike up conversation with the traveler next to me. I go with my gut instinct on this, and it has very rarely steered me wrong. This early morning flight was no exception. I chose to engage with exactly the right person. To this day we call ourselves family and have a bond, created on a three-hour flight, that will not be broken. Never. I call her 'The Woman On The Plane' because it is so hard to explain to my blood family, how these relationships happen for me. But they do, and they change my life, they change how I think, how I feel, how I look at the world. And now they all know exactly who she is.

We talked of many things, family, relationships, lives interrupted, and as I write this I do not know how all those topics came to pass, but it was easy to talk to her. It still is. She is a Breast Cancer survivor, a Kidney Cancer survivor. She lost her brother, her friend, her cousin. She was flying north that day to support her son, her family, when they needed her.

I was struggling with a decision. Taking a deep breath and knowing somehow she was the right person, I told her what the genetic test had revealed and asked for her advice. Do I remove even more healthy organs from my body? I inquire, I had already had the hysterectomy. Do I opt for silicone replacements, sometimes a risky alternative? Or do I take the chance, an eighty-seven percent chance, of being diagnosed myself? What would you do, I ask her, knowing what you do about the treatments, the results, the process? Would you go the prophylactic, preventive route, or would you risk it and hope for early diagnosis? She hesitates only for a fraction of a second. Do it, she said. Do it. There were tears in her eyes.

We have been sending emails back and forth every few days since that flight to the North Country. Months later we are getting together and neither of us can wait. I have loved her from that moment, somehow. She calls me her daughter, and I am. How could we be seated together out of all those people, going to the same place at the same time? We were meant to meet, to influence and help each other along our perspective paths. Either you believe in these things or you don't, and I have friends who go both ways. I respect both beliefs. For me, I have been placed with more than one person who was so impactful on my life it takes my breath away. Conversations that forever changed me, made me think, allowed me to remember. It is not simple chance. It is not blind luck. It is not mere coincidence.

She lost her Mom shortly after we met. I knew what that felt like and hope I helped her through the loss. Decades and miles apart, it is the same. It is your Mom. I struggle with my father's dementia; she knows what to say. With certain people there is a level of acceptance that makes you want to hold onto them and never let go. So, I say, go with that feeling. Don't let them go. They are rare; it is rare to meet them. In this life, you need just a few of these people. Nurture those relationships.

On a plane, you can have conversations with nothing to lose; you can expose yourself, you can be yourself, you can tell your story and meet someone with just as good a story, just as interesting a life, or more so. It has rarely failed me. We have all sat next to the person who is not worth getting to know. If and when that happens, read your book, close your eyes. But when you sit next to a human being who is worth knowing, worth looking in the eye, it is obvious. It is rewarding. It can be amazing.   Learn from them.

Regardless of intention I am living in Plattsburgh; for all the right reasons, my family needs me and I need them.   As I gaze out my window upon arrival, the last of the fall color glows and I am impressed once more with Mother Nature's talents. It's a beautiful place to be.

OCTOBER 16, 2017

At the last minute I hopped on the ferry and attended a Breast Cancer Awareness event where, unbeknownst to me, both of my surgeons were speaking, together. These two smart, real, small, beautiful women talked about options and breast removal and conducted a one-hour presentation on mastectomy and reconstruction. They spoke with a sense of humor, a sense of reality and a sense of compassion.

Near the back of the narrow conference room, a woman two chairs to my right was restless, her legs crossed and uncrossed, her foot swung in a nervous rhythm. She is probably fifteen years younger than me, and sits alone. They are the A-team, I tell her, referring to our speakers. Yes, she says, tears in her eyes. Wish we didn't need them, I say. Yes, she said again, the tears welling up, spilling down one cheek. I reached out and touched her hand. She had been diagnosed, and I never will be. The tears spilled down my cheeks as well, for her, for my opportunity to prevent ever feeling what she feels. I will never feel what 330,000 women each year in this country feel, when they are diagnosed with Breast Cancer. I am overwhelmed with the emotions in that room, the strong women in that room. And the men, I remind myself, equally devastating for the men.

There are strong people everywhere at this conference, some clearly in the midst of treatments, others part of the fight against the disease. All somehow affected and determined to help solve the mystery, assist the victims, educate the families, celebrate the survivors. I discover Dragonheart Vermont, a wonderful, energetic group of survivors and supporters who Race Dragonboats, giant row boats, all over the nation. I vow to join them when I am able.

NOVEMBER 5, 2017

My first appointment with my Plastic Surgeon; it is important to note once again that I never thought I would have a Plastic Surgeon. She was tiny and pregnant, an incongruous combination. I had seen her before, and told her so. I noticed you that day too, she said, and wondered about you.

We are on a journey, the surgeon explains. She is a young, demonstrative, caring bundle of energy that examines me through thin-rimmed glasses. She draws on me in dark purple, talking a little to me, mostly to herself. Hmmm, she comments, yours are a little asymmetrical. We can fix that, she observes. I laugh. Will they ever sag? Never, she replied, they'll be beautiful. I will make them beautiful for you, better than the originals. I like my originals, I say. Of course you do, she replied, looking directly into my eyes. You are making the right choice, she told me. I know, I reply. This is a journey; she reiterated; we will be in touch for years.

Her office is expansive, with too many doors to know where you are. It looks like any other doctor's office except there are silicone and saline rounds, implants, on the counter next to the sink, on a cart in the hallway, in the waiting room. I touch them, pick them up, examine them, knowing two of these will be part of me, someday. They are foreign and feel heavy. I squeeze, wondering if that is what mine might feel like to someone else. The next morning, I squeeze my original parts in the shower, still wondering, trying to determine if they feel the same.

'They will never sag' becomes one of my battle cries, the bright side, the glass half full, even when, for weeks after surgery, I cannot reach above my shoulder for the glass.

JUNE 1

Summer has arrived! I have been sleeping only on my back for eleven weeks. Eighty days, almost three months of not even being able to roll onto my side, which is how I slept for the first forty-eight years of my life, if I recall correctly. I breathe in, sit up in bed, which is much less painful than even a couple of weeks ago.

The next procedure, June eighteenth, will surely keep me on my back and starts another six weeks of lifting and activity restrictions, but there are no drains and it is outpatient, I go home the same day!

JUNE 9

I might have had one extra glass of wine last night. What that means is-- I had one too many glasses of wine last night. Sometimes when I start drinking good wine with good friends I find it hard to stop drinking good wine. And then, sometimes we can switch to not-as-good wine and I won't even notice. At any rate, I awaken this morning with teeth sticking to my lips. Bathroom, lemon water, better.

As I walk back into my room I brush against the doorway, equilibrium and balance still not perfect due to last evening's overindulgence. Here's the thing; I do not *feel* myself brush against the doorway, I *see* myself brush against the doorway. This is the most disturbing effect of my surgery. The nerve endings are gone. In the shower, for example, water and soap runs across my chest but there is no sensation. Hard to describe even, really. When I pull a bag of groceries to my body I know it's there, but I cannot feel it, only a ghost-like pressure that there is something between me and the bag. In reality it is simply the new me. I dig deeply to better describe that feeling, and fail thus far. I keep contemplating it. When I strike a yoga pose that brings my chest down to my thighs it feels completely different than it used to. The new normal.

As I discussed before, this loss is a daily reminder. And not a negative one, because I am alive and healthy and happy and fortunate. This morning it strikes me particularly, that while we can give the illusion of natural breasts with silicone implants and careful surgery, something will always be missing; Mother Nature cannot be exactly replicated. This is good news. Mother Nature should be emulated, awed, admired, respected, not replicated.

So many things in life are trade-offs, decisions that we analyze (or not), choices that we make. We balance these things, trying to determine which is the better path, which has more value in the long run.

Both surgeons told me I would have no feeling, no sensation, after the mastectomy. They scrape all the cells away, including the nerve cells, in order to prevent the cancer. With my particular style, all my exterior parts remain, including the nipples, which are generally removed with mastectomy. There is a chance that a bit of sensory perception may return, but there is no rhyme or reason, no predictability. I knew this was my trade-off and accepted it as one of the few negative results, one of the few downsides.

Occasionally, randomly, there is a twinge. Like someone snapping you with a rubber band, one of the nurses described. Yes, I replied, it is like that! They think those are the nerves showing themselves, she said, healing or returning. No guarantees; never any guarantees that it will get better, but it's a good sign. My circulation and healing has progressed perfectly.

JUNE 10

Poke-O-Moonshine Mountain, I love that name, is a fantastic old mound with sheer granite cliffs celebrated in the rock climbing world. I drive south on the Northway a couple of times a month; this makes me laugh as it's counterintuitive that you can drive south on the Northway.

I go early in the morning, and revel in the twelve-hundred-foot elevation gain of this Adirondack legend. The half bald peak has a survey marker, a fire-lookout tower, and the views of the North Country are exceptionally breathtaking. East across Lake Champlain to the Green Mountains, West to the High Peaks and Whiteface, south to Giant and beyond. North toward the Canadian border there is lake after lake and rolling hill after rolling hill.

I do not ever tire of the view, and always climb as far up on the tower as is allowed, it's been a lookout for over one hundred and fifty years, you know the views are good! The wind can come up and surprise you but most mornings are peaceful, most mornings I am the only person there. On the south face the granite is precipitous, the cliff drops a few hundred feet down into deciduous forest, and there are perfect granite chairs carved into the rock by Mother Nature, comfortably concave. I have become a creature of habit here and nearly always choose the same indentation for my seat, gazing slightly southeast, toward the sun if there is any, toward the Lake. Toward the water view.

The hike up Poke-O-Moonshine was my maternal grandparents first date. Pearl and Don were married in 1932, so while we're not exactly sure when the first date was, it was sometime in the roaring 20's. No wonder I have a connection to that sacred ground, no wonder I feel at home there, am compelled to go back to the same place rather than explore the myriad of other peaks and valleys in America's largest State Park.

There is something comforting about such a routine, about going back to your roots. With my new lease on life I also have a renewed love of this mountain. I hike down the long trail, cross the beaver dam, hike back up, and then down the way I came. I like to think the feeling is the same as a century ago when my ancestors explored here. There is a patch of old growth forest remaining, and those solemn trunks have now witnessed four generations of our family.

As I write this I remember June tenth is my parent's anniversary, 1961, a marriage that lasted twenty-five years, almost to the day. My father fell out of love with my mother and into the arms of another woman. It was originally a bitter separation for me, but I have come to love my stepmother with conviction. In fact, she is an angel, caring for my father when seeing him is incredibly difficult, when he is not quite the man he used to be. She spends hours at his side, kissing him like she always did and comforting him in ways I cannot.

For a long time, there was uncertainty in our relationship; for the middle decade I would tell her that I love her, because that is what my family does, we express that every chance we get, and she would say Thank You. Nothing more, nothing less. Just Thank You. In the last half decade, after nearly thirty years married to my father, she tells me she loves me. She and I are forever bonded by the experiences of the last two years.

I don't think I get attached to things, I don't know why, she told me this past winter, shrugging. You may be lucky in that, I reply, meaning every word. We are all cut from a different cloth.

JUNE 12

My eyes squint in the bright sunshine, a rare commodity here. I wake up flat on my back as I have since March seventh. No other option with those expanders, I assure you. We are piled on my side of the bed, myself and the two Beagles, just the way we like it. At least this morning they are not wet.

My slight headache is far outweighed by the wonderful feeling that friendship leaves in each of us. While I am officially without a partner in my life right now, I'm not even close to being alone or lonely. Last night we had half a dozen friends over for dinner, and wine, and more wine, and a roaring fire and, most importantly, companionship, conversation. Friendships are not easy to find, to maintain, to nurture. I treasure them, and try to convey to those special people how special they are, every chance I get.

My Friend Basket. I describe this by holding out my hand, fingers curled, palm up. My Friend Basket is a sacred place, a powerful place. It contains people who you may talk to every week, and you may talk to every year. But those people, if you called them, would come. There are not many in there. They are the best people I know. I am one of the best people they know. It is a place of mutual respect and love and acceptance that you have with less than a dozen people in your life, such a small percentage of the world and yet so important!

I woke up this morning knowing that I am a good friend and I have good friends. While we think we can survive alone, and we can, it's better when you don't have to, don't choose to. Out of a hundred-plus contacts on my phone, my Friend Basket stands out. Even when they say they are going to call and they don't call, and I say I'm going to call and I don't call, there is no less love, no less respect. Sometimes I send a message just making sure they are OK, they do the same to me. There is no pressure; when the time is right we fully reconnect. We come together just like we left off. It may not be forever. A couple of years ago this slightly corny saying went around— "People come into our realms for 'A Reason, A Season or A Lifetime'...I believe this to be true. We learn from them, they learn from us, and they either stay or move on.

If you have met people who have no Friend Basket, you should feel sorry that they do not have, or give, that love and support.

JUNE 16

We load up coolers in the early afternoon and head south two hours to Saratoga Springs. Saratoga Performing Arts Center (SPAC) is like no other venue. Open to the air with a genius design that allows the lawn seats direct visual to the stage, we go as often as we can, but not often enough as life races by. For the last few years as we approached fifty, and those of you in my generation know this, the bands we grew up on are touring the country! In this case, Foreigner and Whitesnake. Journey has come through, Joan Jett, Def Leopard, many more. It makes me laugh as I write this. Watching them was amazing, they must be in their 70's, sound great, look a bit old, their hair is mostly gray, what's left of it.

The SPAC concerts allow us to step back in time. They are fantastic. Next month Chicago and REO Speedwagon team up, Ronnie Milsap plays the County Fair. Last year that stage held the Charlie Daniels Band—at eighty-two he is absolutely amazing, on both vocals and fiddle.

A few weeks ago I was sitting at the counter in a friend's house, there are six of us, one fifteen years my junior. Who's Foreigner? she asks innocently. The question is met by silence, then amazement. Oh, Foreigner! she recovers, laughing awkwardly. Another friend quips—we almost had to vote you off the island! We laugh. We tell her the song titles she would know, and she does, although they are before her time. Foreigner 4. My generation knows every word to that album, it was one of my first records, back when we called them records, not vinyl. Who the heck renamed records 'vinyl'? It's still a record to me. My brother has milk crates full of them in the basement, and we keep threatening to have a party with his two turntables (yes, turntables) from the late 80's and simply rock the night away. I wonder if that will ever happen.

We dance at weddings, to the music of the 80's, like we're still twenty-one. We contemplate how we can possibly remember all those lyrics when we cannot recollect what we did yesterday. Another mystery.

These concerts also allow us to remember, or not remember, how old we are, and also remember that age is a state of mind indeed. How old would you be if you didn't know how old you are?

My Mom listened to country music, now super old school country; Charlie Pride, Glen Campbell, Lynn Anderson, Patsy Cline, Loretta Lynn, John Denver. I know all the words to those albums, too, and keep them in my brain for Sunday mornings, played now on Pandora, not vinyl.

JUNE 17

Father's Day. Each of these holidays remind us that there are not many more. They are happy and somber affairs. When you ask him what he wants to eat, the answer is predictable and All-American; steak. The Nursing Home has a small back patio that is utilized mostly by us and our unquenchable family desire to be outside.

We take over all the wrought iron tables and I have a chance to Cater, part of my ex-life that I truly miss. Catering to my family is extra special. We bring wine and appetizers and make an event out of it. So great to be together and not inside the austere, sad walls of this place.

For months after I moved to New York I would tell people I was here because he was not well. I was trying to be, what, politically correct? Delicate? Not really my style. I don't know why that was my answer, frankly. Anyway, now I simply tell them that my father is dying. This is the truth. The cold, hard, truth. And it eliminates most people's follow-up questions that used to be, next time I saw them, how's your father doing? I never knew the to answer that one, it silenced me, and now I do. I have never been one of those folks who simply say 'good' every time someone asks how they are.

After dinner this particular day we load the dishes and Catering equipment into my Stepmother's car instead of my own. My brother and I drive to the Ferry dock, to Burlington and the Hope Lodge. My apprehension has grown exponentially that this surgery will be similar to the first. And it is, in a way. Utilizing the same incisions, my plastic surgery team is taking out the expanders and replacing them with permanent silicone implants. The recovery from the first surgery was tough, but there is light at the end of the tunnel.

Our original plan for the evening was to walk the beautiful mile downtown; you pass mansions and huge hardwood trees, and grab a cocktail on Church Street. Too many festivities over the weekend, too many thoughts in our brains, we pour the ever-present if prohibited wine into red solo cups and hope (pun intended) that sleep will come.

JUNE 18

It's a do-over, I text my soul mate. 6am check-in, surgery. For the third and final time. I awaken two hours before I need to and watch the summer sky gradually lighten, just days before the solstice this is around four am. I can see tall thin maple trees outside the window swaying in a warm, humid windstorm. The thick brick walls insulate me from the sound and the feeling. Like watching a silent movie, I cannot hear the wind, cannot feel the temperature. I am simply an observer. For once, my mind does not drift, I soak in the sight.

Propped up by the pillows, my view is uphill to the hospital, from here you can watch tiny people come and go. I wonder why they are in the same place I am, what path they are on.

The last two years of my life, I have become incredibly introspective. Perhaps I ponder it too much, wondering about so many things and the timing of them all. The irony strikes me; we have less control than we want to believe over our lives, yet I have made drastic choices, taken drastic measures, to control my destiny.

We walk to the hospital on the same sidewalk, the sun already far above the horizon. This is an outpatient procedure; I imagine that check-in will be a flashback and I am right. The same receptionist greets us in the Third Floor Surgical waiting room. I give her my name and date of birth. She tells us the Operating room is booked for four hours this time. Perfect, I reply. We smile at each other, relieved. Even the familiarity does not completely quell the butterflies.

We feel like regulars; my brother accepts the pager that will tell him I am in recovery. Our favorite registration nurse sends us a perky greeting. The anesthesiologist tells us he has been practicing for fifty years. If you do the math on that perhaps he should already be retired, but he makes us laugh and passes the time.

Only one surgeon this time, same purple magic marker, same style gown. The expanders have done their work and will be replaced by permanent silicone implants this morning. When they wheel me into the operating room I am greeted by beautiful people, all women, most of whom I am very familiar with.

I move onto the table, wide awake this time as we chat about an odd assortment of things, they put me at ease. The atmosphere is much different, not so dire, not so serious. This is the last step, this takes me back to my normal life, back to feeling whole; it starts me on the path to accepting the new me. Today I get The New Girls.

Everything goes perfectly. I awaken slowly in recovery, frightened to move, frightened that the pain will be even a fraction of what it was last time. I focus, I breathe. There is a level of discomfort but nothing like the first round! I am so relieved tears well up in my eyes. My brother squeezes my hand, asks me what I need. Nothing, I say. I'm great.

I am wrapped in a vice-like Velcro vest that stifles my breath, but only a little. Still all good, so much easier than the first surgery! So much easier, so much less painful. The exact same incisions are used and sewn up in her perfectionist style. No drains, no bandages. The four-hour procedure leaves me with few complaints except the six weeks of restrictions. No lifting, no yoga, no strenuous anything. Seems like an eternity, but it's not. I breathe.

I smile at her, **my** plastic surgeon, thinking she wears a size zero and I have **never** worn a size zero in my life. Ever. And I never will, and I'm fine with that. She tried six different sizes of implants before she was satisfied that she had made the right decision. Before they put me under I had reminded her that she had promised me beautiful. My Mom chimes into my brain; beauty is in the eye of the beholder. Yes, Mom.

The final surgical touches are done with the aforementioned liposuction to move around a little fatty tissue and make things smooth, more natural looking, done at the discretion of the surgeon. They call it 'fat grafting' but I cannot tell anyone I have undergone 'fat grafting.'! Liposuction?! I had asked her, add it to the growing list of things I never, in my wildest imagination, thought I would experience. It's a bonus, she tells me in post-op. We laugh. Most people who have that pay a lot of money for it, they don't exercise, she tells me, they take the easy way out.

The procedure causes the only bruising that I have experienced through the whole process, but still nothing like you might imagine, minimal at best. I can live with that; there is light at the end of the tunnel. I welcome The New Girls.

Eight hours later I am home in my bed. Elation is the only word that comes to mind. I am elated to be done with surgery and the hospital. The pure relief at how much more comfortable I am after this procedure brings tears to my eyes, literally, again, wow, the relief. They prescribe me painkillers which I do not need this time. Tylenol and Melatonin get me through the first few days and then I don't even require those to get my rest.

My biggest fear had been waking up and having to talk myself into moving, brace myself to use my core and pectorals. As summer comes to the North Country I gaze out the window and look forward to everything.

JUNE 19

I wake up suddenly, as always on my back, excited at this first day of the rest of my life. The New Girls are strapped into a compression undergarment like you cannot imagine, with extra adjustments and Velcro to stop even the faintest movement. Not sexy but it keeps them in place, does not touch the twelve inches of incisions and reminds me I'm to stay fairly immobile until August first.

August first I am calling my free day. Free of all restrictions, free from worry, free from appointments for a while. Free to move on. The 'fat-grafting' was done on my stomach and my flanks (I thought only horses had flanks....) and results in me having to wear, prior to the Spanx, the largest one-size fits all compression gizmo that I have ever seen around my waist and hips. A full eighteen inches wide, and a little scratchy, this somehow becomes an extension of me over the next few weeks, to keep all the disturbed parts in place and fabulous.

It is nearly twice as long as it needs to be, so the giant Velcro flap is constantly sticking to things and causing trouble. The learning curve on that is about three days after which I don't need my brother's help on how and where to arrange it properly. John, I call out to him, for the first two days, laughing, which way does this go?! As I read that sentence it sounds ridiculous, but it's true and makes me laugh. Sometimes it is the little things in life that make us stumble the hardest. This item is equally not sexy!

I'll be able to tell if you don't wear them, the surgeon warns me, and I believe her. The incisions and the muscles of the chest are a bit tender. None of this matters and is barely even a consideration because I am in no pain, just the slightest discomfort. Certainly friends and family are tired of hearing how much easier this procedure was. The relief, and I know I am being redundant here, brings tears to my eyes. There is a light at the end of the tunnel. Bright, sunshiny light.

Time in a hospital has once again put things into perspective. You can always find people, many people, worse off than you are. Instead of feeling sorry for myself I see the heart surgery patient, the child with MS, the lung cancer survivor and the accident victim. I feel great, I am one of the lucky ones.

The down side of feeling this good is that I am ready to get back into my life and all that it entails. Patience is a virtue I do not possess. I breathe, I write, I research. I feel like me.

SUMMER SOLSTICE

An even stronger windstorm this evening is swaying our own maple trees, and the open windows allow all of my senses to work. It begins to rain and the sound is mesmerizing. It takes me back to the cabin of my childhood, steadily pounding on the metal roof. How I love to sleep to the sound of rain.

In Western Colorado, there is little rain and when it comes it tends to drench you, Monsoon style, in the late afternoon. Rarely is there a steady, thrumming, life-giving rain. When I left New York I had no use for it, now I embrace it with a passion that surprises me.

As this particular night progresses the showers vary in intensity, increasing each time as if from a distance. Two or three owls converse around our home, adding to the mystery, the lure of the woods. It is a beautiful celebration of the Solstice, longest day of the year, allowing me to enjoy the first warm night of the season, windows wide open, curtains flowing.

My Poke-O-Moonshine (did I tell you I love that name?) grandparents had a summer home on the Great Sacandaga Reservoir in the southern part of the range toward Albany. The Camp itself sat on a small bay and from the Adirondack chairs on the front porch we were often able to watch the thunderstorms come down the lake. As the line of rain got closer and closer it was nearly always accompanied by impressive lightning and booming thunder. We sat with my grandfather, fascinated, counting the distance it was from us in seconds, doing the translation to miles away.

Tonight the wind in the full green leaves of summer is nearly as good; resonant, strong, more variable. Crickets, peepers and tree frogs. Mother Nature's amazing chorus. Celebrate the little things.

JUNE 25

Post-op. Do you like them? Are they too big? the surgeon inquires anxiously. We have developed a relationship on this journey and the answer is important; it's important to her that I am happy. I do like them, I answer her, I trust your judgment, but they are bigger than I wanted.

I know, I tried six different sizes, she tells me, I made them even! You were asymmetrical, she reminds me gently, and I laugh at her candor. These are the best size; you have big shoulders; these are the best, she repeats, nodding, smiling. Even you cannot perfectly duplicate Mother Nature, I tell her, equally candid. You know I still think you are a rock star. We laugh.

The New Girls are arranged a bit differently on my frame. They are separated further than the originals and protrude just slightly on either side, so that when I reach forward close to my body, I can feel them on the inside of my arms. As I sit in her office my recollection is vague as to how the Original Girls even felt.

JULY 4

My friend and I are watching the crowd at the fireworks show on the Fourth of July; observing the diversity, enjoying the energy. We are on the grass surrounded by local patriots who, every year, make the pilgrimage here, to sit on the banks of the Saranac River and watch the sky. Together we celebrate our Independence; on this day perhaps we are a unified nation.

This particular evening, one of my only public appearances since the surgeries, I am wearing a simple tank top. Not a big deal in America, right? For me, this first time out with The New Girls, it's huge. Always conscious of the way I look, tonight that sense is off the chart. Of course, no one notices but me. Would you know if you didn't know? No. I breathe and quell the butterflies.

Some of those patriots are showing us a lot of skin that we would, well, rather not see. You know what I mean. That is not sexy, I say, laughing. So not sexy, we are all laughing. We are together.

Not sexy is one of my standard expressions. I use it to comment on odd things that happen, mistakes, awkwardness, about anything really, that takes you by surprise, perhaps embarrasses you a little, perhaps takes you back to a moment in time when you were not feeling all that sexy.

Previously, I would not have considered what I have done sexy, not in my wildest imagination. But perhaps it is. Because sexy is not just physical characteristics, it is a presence. It is a confidence, it is a style, a way of presenting oneself, regardless of appearance. Remember when I got the compliment about being real? Well, it's sexy to be real, and this is about as real as it gets.

Sexy is when someone looks you in the eye and finds you interesting. Those glances can be sideways on a plane, at the grocery store, anywhere, and often when you least expect it. Sexy is strength in the face of adversity. Sexy is knowing what to say when knowing what to say is damn hard. Sexy is when someone speaks with an easy, calm demeanor that says, I got this, even when the situation is out of their control. Sexy is being there when someone needs you.

Smart is the new sexy; intelligence is very important to me. The ability to admit when you are wrong, admit when you simply don't know the answer. That vulnerability is sexy. That honesty is sexy.

Sexy is quiet undeniable genius in an incredible, generous human being hidden behind an untrimmed beard, uncombed hair and stained t-shirts. He is one of my best friends, and always will be.

Sexy is saying, with a shrug, you know who I am, take it or leave it, I'm not changing. That's sexy, that's confident.

Your walk is almost a strut, a friend told me once; I raised my eyebrows at him. My walk is, indeed, confident. It's sexy because physically, I am not beautiful; my walk is a part of me that I like, and it has helped me on this journey. My walk, my attitude, my presence, has taken me places with people that I never would have met, never would have loved, never would have learned from.

Sexy is an unexpected attraction that takes you somewhere you would never have gotten had you hesitated, had you not said yes. Sexy is being willing to take the risk.

JULY 6

When the weather in the North Country is bad, it's intolerable. When it's good, it is downright incredible. We are having a week of low humidity, blue skies, forty shades of green foliage, flowers blooming everywhere, nearly always a breeze. Simply awesome.

And today I am on a pilgrimage of sorts. After eight months, I will once again see the Woman on the Plane. She and her husband have rented a house two hours west and invited me to visit. We have been in touch weekly if not daily since we were seated together last November. When her invitation came there was no hesitation on my part; the bond is strong and will remain strong, hopefully forever.

Remember where I reside; how many tiny roads there are? Even Google Maps gets confused. There is a bridge out that the folks in California don't know about so I wander for a while, pick some orange Adirondack Lilies for my hostess. Google redirects me four times back to the missing bridge. An extra hour on a day like this, seeing things have never seen, is a gift, not a hassle, and makes me laugh as I have no sense of which way I should be going. For the 30th time I wish I had a road Atlas. Never used to leave home without it! Google has successfully directed me thousands of miles back and forth across this country and through major cities without fail, telling me about traffic accidents that just happened, moments ago. They don't know this bridge is out?! And will be, by the looks of it, for months? I laugh again. Welcome to the North Country. Probably not enough people affected by and utilizing this county road to update the information. It's a lesson and when I get home I put the very worn and slightly outdated fifty state Road Atlas back in my car. I know you remember those. I finally circumnavigate the bridge closure and find Trout Lake.

After years of wandering the planet now I simply leave myself a window of arrival time. Between five and six, I said, hoping for the best. Windows give you an opportunity for neither party to be wrong. This allows me to arrive on time, if only by the slimmest margin. Oh yeah, my host tells me, the bridge. I was hoping you weren't coming that way.

She greets me perfectly, with a huge hug reserved for those closest to us and that lasts. We are privileged to feel so connected. To have made this rare connection. I meet 'her Bill' whose story I already know, and it's a good, solid love story and he is a rock-solid guy. The rental house is beautiful, hanging on the edge of the water with an assortment of decks and bedrooms built into the granite shelf. We watch the sun set, wine in hand, and talk, talk, talk. She is intuitive and as much of a character as I recalled her to be. We laugh at the things we experience, the world and the people in it. Laughter is such a great thing.

We get outside of nearly three bottles of wine and some steaks. It's midnight before we are done learning about each other for today. Do people come into your life for a reason, a season or a lifetime? Who knows?

The next day her daughter, close to my age, arrives and I depart. As I drive away I wonder if I should have taken the opportunity to tell her how special her Mom is. How she should take every opportunity to spend time with her, how she should, perhaps, make sure she says what needs to be said, does what needs to be done. But who am I to give that advice? I am jealous that she still has a Mom she can talk to, see, do things with. Envious may be a better word. Clearly, as I write this those thoughts have stayed with me.

When I arrive at my next destination and discuss these feelings with my friend she tells me it was not my place to intervene. Not my place to give unsolicited advice. I still waver on this decision, and perhaps if I see her daughter again, I will, indeed, tell her how great her mom is, and how much I miss my own. The older I get the less I seem to know, but I know that. While perhaps some of the lessons that we learn are too late, they are lessons nonetheless. We grow from them, we move forward.

JULY 7

Appreciate the little things.   People who have faced adversity appreciate small pleasures the most.   This is a blanket statement and I know those can be dangerous.   I find this one to be true the majority of the time.

People who get upset about little things have not had big, bad, sad things happen to them or the ones they love.   They have not held their mother's hand when she drew her last breath.   Those kind of things change you, forever, so that when there's a bad slow driver in front of you or your quarter gets sucked into the vending machine it simply does not matter. It does not make you upset, you just accept what is, you solve the problem as best you can, you move on.

I arrive at a friend's camp in Western New York.   We are talking about The New Girls as they are such a curiosity, for people who love me and people who don't.   It's pretty drastic, I say, casually, putting my legs up on the picnic table.   It's very drastic! she exclaims, straightening in her seat.   Very drastic! This silences me. After months of introspection and healing, I have become used to what I have done.   We gaze out at the water, each lost in our own thoughts, our own experiences.

To the vast majority of the rest of the world it is incredibly drastic, almost unthinkable.   In fact, this Friend Basket member has confided in me that she would not have made my choice.   She is steadfast in her support, but would have chosen the more traveled path; watch and wait.   You always take the less traveled path she jokes with me now.   Indeed I do, I laugh, sometimes it's hard to find.

To our absolute amazement that evening there is a full-on, professional fireworks show at this tiny lake in the middle of nowhere on the end of a dead end road. Of course we are drinking wine, the sky is clear, we are sitting out by the campfire. We applaud and laugh and are thrilled to be in the right place at the right time. The fireworks are donated, they are beautiful.

We ask a neighbor who makes it happen. The neighbor replies, with a shrug, they do it every year. His voice is puzzled, nearly annoyed at our fascination with and appreciation of something so ordinary. It is not ordinary to us, our first year, our perspectives. What a great surprise!

Appreciate the little things.

JULY 8

Another little butterfly is in my stomach. I am changing at my friend's camp, changing into a bathing suit for the first time, my bikini bathing suit. I am nervous, I am critical, looking in the mirror. Taking a deep breath, I step out into the living room area, my friend stands in the kitchen. If you didn't know, you wouldn't know, would you? I ask the badly worded question with trepidation, hesitation, angst. The New Girls are a secret for the most part, only a select few of my Friend Basket know what I have done. That's how I want it, it's the conversation I had with my surgeons, with everyone.

I badly want my transformation to not be physically obvious, to be my interesting secret. At this point in the journey, I notice little else about myself. As I catch glimpses of me in a window, mirror, anywhere, The New Girls are my focus. Do people know? This makes my inquiry, and my friend's answer, very important. Am I still sexy?

She and I have a relationship based on honesty, which is rare and treasured. She will tell me the hard things, the things I don't want to hear, and I do the same. We are allowed to give the unsolicited advice spoken about earlier. Not even all the members of my Friend Basket can do that. But we can, and it creates a deep trust and deep comfort, knowing she will always tell me the truth.

You look great, she says, you wouldn't know. I breathe. Wandering back to the mirror, we are in agreement. No one would know if they didn't know. So as my path continues, only those I choose will, indeed, know. The irony is not lost on me that I am writing all this in a book.

It is an amazingly beautiful day and my cares are back at home. I take the kayak out, pick water lilies, help with dinner, drink a beer, meet some genuine wonderful relatives and friends of friends, drink another beer. Even The New Girls feel much more comfortable.

I drive home along the northern edge of the United States, within sight of the St. Lawrence Seaway and Canada. With little traffic and low speed limits, my late afternoon drive east is memorable. I stop in at a winery and taste, their wines are drinkable and interesting. I spend more than I should and feel excellent about it, supporting a local business. Working late on a Sunday the owners are manning the store, as small business owners often have to do in order to succeed, survive, prosper.

JULY 10

My post-op appointment is scheduled early afternoon and the drive is fantastic. My brother accompanies me and we opt to take the road north to the Canadian Border and drive the bridges rather than take the ferry; we have the time and are looking for a change of scenery. It is incredibly green with black and white Holstein cows and crops and baby animals everywhere dotting the fields. It's a good day to be alive.

We arrive on time and wait for a quarter of an hour or so, which is unusual in this practice. When I am admitted to the exam room my favorite PA enters. I feel fine, I tell her, but there is a soft spot that reminds me of the fluid buildup after the original surgery and it concerns me.

I don't know how the implants should feel, honestly. They are brand new to me, I want to like them, I want them to be perfect.

She glances my way, a crease on her forehead and for once I see some stress in the office, some tension. Every other time the appointments are peaceful, slow-paced. How are you? I inquire, my sixth sense knowing the answer. I have seen her many times this spring and know she is out of sorts. It has been a rough week, she replies and begins my exam. She carefully scrutinizes the spot in question. It's part of the implant, she explains, bulging just a little bit under the arm.

To my complete surprise, she steps back and looks at me, hands outstretched. You have nipples! And you are whole! she cries, steadying herself by drawing in a long breath. You are the best case I have seen in days.

Our eyes meet, my face flushes with embarrassment as realization dawns and I rush to explain myself. I get it, I tell her, I'm sorry. I understand now. I am being too particular. This was my choice. It was elective. I know you see so much worse, so much suffering and uncertainty. I get it. That's why I chose to do this. I've seen it happen to people I loved, I have seen them suffer. I know, I'm sorry. She smiles at me, and with this confession we are bonded, at the same time I am ashamed. This team works mainly with cancer patients, a lot of cancer patients. They make their lives better, put them back together when Mother Nature betrays them with that disease.

The little protrusion, little soft spot I will always have is simply that, a harmless part of the silicone implant that is not quite as smooth as the rest of the results. This conversation will stay with me a very long time and I want to share it.

That same day, when my brother and I left the office, a small child with severe facial disfigurement held the door for us. For us. The reality was very impactful to me; I am truly one of the lucky ones. I had the time and the place and the opportunity to change my life, potentially save my life. Not everyone does.

Here in the Americas Breasts are a bit of a mystery. We cover them up instead of showing them off proudly at the beach as they do in much of Europe. Most women wear padded bras so the nipples don't show through their t-shirts. We strap the Girls down so they don't sway when we walk. While cleavage is trendy, the bare naked female breast is something that we avert our eyes from. Perhaps the mystery is a good thing as I don't suppose I want to see them all, either, but the human body is basically the same for everyone, we all start out with the same parts.

At my first appointment with the plastic surgeon I told her I wanted perfect New Girls and that I never want to have to wear a bra again. Never. The eyebrows shot up. Really? she asked. I laughed. Really, I reply. This conversation took place to cover up my nervousness, to mask my hesitation of opting for extensive surgery when I don't even take Advil. It's the second upside, the first upside is such limited risk, the third upside is never another mammogram! And I know, they're not perfect. But they are never going to sag.

This evening I open a great bottle of wine and go through my underwear drawer, removing the bras, tossing the worn ones, saving the ones that could be of use to someone. Someone else. There are a few beautiful lacy ones that still have the tags. They fit The New Girls and my conservative side puts them back in the drawer. My free side takes them out again and puts them into the pile for someone else.

JULY 14

My relief at the ease of the second procedure has morphed into pure joy in the decision I made. Pure joy. True Relief. The breast surgeon cautions me that there is still a tiny bit of Breast Cancer risk. No one can ever get all the cells, she tells me, hand on my arm. More important to me and at the forefront of my mind is that we successfully decreased my risk by around eighty-five percent. Remember my friend that said it was a 'no-brainer?' The BRCA2 Genetic Mutation indicates a risk of eighty-seven percent over a lifetime. By taking this action, I reduced it by eighty-five percent. I was not willing to live with the option of early detection, because my fear of a Cancer diagnosis, any type of Cancer, is palpable. Causes those butterflies. 'The C word' we call it. My family and Friend Basket knows exactly what that means.

You're younger than the average age your family is diagnosed; one geneticist had said to me. And if we catch it early, we can cure it to a large extent. I stare at her, wide-eyed. But then I would have CANCER, I reply, the 'C' word. How could she know exactly what that means to me? That it would feel like a death sentence? While my practical side knows some types can be cured, my life has been altered by cancer. It is my biggest fear. It is one of my only fears. And allow me to reiterate, it's a big one.

We all know someone who has been taken by Cancer. In many instances it is someone that we loved; in some instances, it is someone that we loved tremendously, someone who gave us life.

You are the bravest person I know, one friend said to me. While I am stunned into silence at this tremendous compliment, I firmly disagree with her. The bravest people we know have met cancer head on and fought it, battling for a chance to continue life with advice from doctors that is terrifying and treatments that are poison. They are the bravest people I know. My family and friends, countless others, have experienced this. Hundreds of thousands a year battle for their lives, they did not have a choice. I decided. I would make the same decision again.

'My mother would have done anything to live', this is a quote from *Pretty is what Changes,* a book by Jessica Queller; she made the same decision I have. This quote resonated with me more than any other. My mother, too, would have done anything to live.

JULY 17

YES! I feel fabulous, I tell my plastic surgeon. Went kayaking yesterday! I am pleased with my progress.

The reprimand is quick and her voice is slightly raised, out of character. You are not listening to me, she says. I don't care if you feel great. Six weeks. Six weeks; she lists off the restrictions again. I mean it, she tells me, again. You'll thank me later. Where's your Velcro?

She hugs me four times during that visit, I hug her back, hard. She is a huge part of a huge transition in my life. I don't need to see her for three months! The light at the end of the tunnel flashes. It's lovely.

JULY 20

A friend invites me to the Eagles Concert in Boston. The Eagles. Eleven rows back. What a great reintroduction to the world. I pack, no bras, decide against the Velcro encumbrances (I know, not following the rules...) and have an absolutely amazing time. It takes me back to my youth, it is a sing-along with twelve thousand other people.

In front of us an elderly woman sits alone beside an empty chair. I know she is one of the brave people, to go anyway, even though her life clearly dealt her a hand she did not want. Her partner is missing from an event that they probably planned for a year or more. Savor every moment, say yes to every opportunity. Life is short.

After the show we drink tequila and talk about the many definitions of sexy, how many uses there are for the word. Sexy is knowing what to say and how to say it. Turns out, some of the time, he does not. He is, however, one of the good guys, and I truly appreciate his friendship and photography skills.

AUGUST 2

I am the sole sponsor of a Susan G. Komen Breast Cancer Golf Tournament. I have a Spice business called Spicing Up The World; this is the second year I have sponsored. It's not about golf, it's about awareness. Being a key part of that is a humbling, rewarding, experience that brings me closer to my family and its struggles, reminds me again how many people are impacted.

This cause is so close to my heart! Even more so now as the Event Director has become such an amazing friend of mine. My mother would have loved these wonderful ladies, this one in particular. She is seventy-nine, a bundle of energy, compassion and ideas. I want to cruise the rivers in Europe, she tells me over our shared passion for Zinfandel. Mostly born and raised here, they have taken me in and supported me in so many ways on this journey.

The Director and another member are two-time Breast Cancer survivors. Twice they received the diagnosis! These are strong women; they are simply amazing. They enjoy life, playing golf most Thursday mornings with us and maintaining their daily activities, savoring every moment. There are several other survivors among our group of just under forty diverse ladies. Everyone knows someone with cancer, everyone is affected. We remember that some do not survive. My mother, aunt and uncle did not survive. This makes our conversations, our relationships, even more precious.

My bottles of Secret Spice Remedy go into the goody bags, go into the spice cupboards, those that try it love it. I auction off my Chef services as well and those super ladies buy tickets with enthusiasm. I am happy to be part of them. There is no financial gain on my part. The entire experience is always positive. I get to be a supporter of a cause that has become universal nationwide, worldwide. Everyone is more aware of Breast Cancer and our fight against it, as people, as a nation, because of Susan G. Komen.

For the first time, after the tournament, I speak in public about my surgery. Astonishing to me, the response is simply quiet. I don't know what I expected, but that wasn't it. All the participants are watching me; they acknowledge me but they hesitate to react. They are surprised, they are undecided, I have breached their comfort zone. I firmly believe they are digesting this information, my story. Some think I am brave; some think it's too drastic. Their background knowledge is limited. Few know of the BRCA genetic indicators; few know of the procedure I chose. After a long half-minute or so (it was long to me, anyway!), there is sincere, heartfelt applause, a support group who will share my story. They are glad they did not have to make my decision, and I am glad for them, it was not an easy path.

This experience also reinforces, absolutely supports, my decision to write this book. I have been a bit incapacitated, more or less, for several months, unable to do things I want to do. Unable, even, to do the things I don't want to do. It is worth it.

When folks I run into politely inquire why, what surgery, are you OK, you seem healthy, and what happened exactly? Why aren't you golfing? Or working, or climbing, or…. any number of things… I draw in a breath, trying to explain. I start by asking, are you familiar with the BRCA genetic test? A huge majority, the vast majority, say no. A wall is instantly built, a hard obstacle to overcome. In most instances I simply tell them it's a long story because the explanation, the situation, is, indeed, lengthy, personal, complicated and to most folks simply too far out of the mainstream.

Openly discussing removing your healthy breasts is a foreign concept for most people, perhaps even counterintuitive; it leaves them with an uncertain feeling because it is a new approach, a new frontier, a new solution. Very importantly, they are not ignorant. There is simply little exposure, little information, few opportunities to learn. We easily discuss lung, stomach, brain; we are just getting comfortable with Breast and Prostrate Cancer.

Months after the tournament, I had lunch with one of these golfers, diagnosed for the first time in 1985. I was embarrassed when I found out, she confided in me, like I had done something wrong. She was diagnosed again many years later. As an acquaintance of hers, you would have no idea. She is quiet, understated, observant, compassionate.

I ask her the same question that I asked The Woman on The Plane. Would you do what I did, I inquire. Yes, she said, nodding, yes, I would.

AUGUST 27

As I grow stronger every day, my father fails before my eyes. His ability to communicate what he feels, wants, needs or questions becomes more and more limited. My resolve is in concrete, let people know what you want before you are unable to convey that information. Let your Friend Basket know what you want. Those you love who love you back will be there when you need them.

I am lucky enough, today, to be in the presence of one of those people, my friend, my soul mate. I have missed seeing her, she always tells me the truth and has an understanding of people that is rare. She flew to New York last August for my hysterectomy and has taken care of me in so many ways I cannot even list them all. She and her amazing husband took me into her home for weeks. Took me into their hearts forever; we have a very special bond. This soul mate, the one beside me this day, I will be in touch with forever. We'll take care of each other forever.

Dueling pistols, that's what we need, I tell her. Just don't miss, she laughs. Don't you miss, I reply, our solution warms our heart because we would be in it together. As we sit on her incredible concrete patio in Western Colorado and contemplate life, we have come up with several such solutions. We want to be able to control our destiny. Far fetched? Impractical? Perfect? Wrong? Wrong for those you leave behind but not wrong for you? There is no right answer.

SEPTEMBER 17

I am back on that beautiful patio in Colorado after spending sixteen days rafting the Grand Canyon. There's a reason it's one of the Seven Wonders of the World. The pictures cannot do it justice, cannot give you the scale, the beauty, the depth, the peace.

Sixteen days of not being connected, I knew only one other person on the trip. Fourteen other strangers are now friends I may never see again. I felt small, insignificant, special, renewed. I felt peace, felt the soul of the place. My relationship with the Grand Canyon and other soulful places is, perhaps, a whole other book.

Tonight my friend hosts a pre-birthday birthday party with a few of the stars in my ex-life. The New Girls are the focus, the intrigue, the fascination. For the umpteenth time, I am determined to tell my story and increase the awareness. Like the others, they have mixed emotions and mixed reactions. They respect my decision; they are glad they did not have to make it themselves. They want to know more.

SEPTEMBER 19

How old would you be if you didn't know how old you are?

Today I turn fifty.   It IS just a number!

I roll from my back onto my left side, experimentally, and gaze out the window at the beginning of the fall colors. I feel like me.

SEPTEMBER 26

I have the honor of accompanying my nephew to a Jeep Jamboree weekend in Maine. This is our second year of this adventure and it is so meaningful to me. He is half my age and, I think, so much wiser than I was at twenty-five. We share entrees at dinner, he reminds me of things I have forgotten, he looks out for me.

In less than a month he will move to Colorado; I feel like he is following in my footsteps, again I am honored. I helped to instill in him a sense of adventure, a sense of exploration, a sense of learning. Without children of my own, it's nice to know I have influenced such a wonderful human being.

He knows of the surgeries and has kept track of me, checking in throughout the process. He is an observer, a thinker. It's important to me that he understands my decision, and he does. Why wouldn't you? he had replied, quizzically, when I asked him if he thought my decision was the right one. He questioned it only when I told him it had been more physically difficult than I had imagined. Was it worth it? Yes, still worth it, we decided, as a team. And it was.

OCTOBER 23

I love the water, any kind of water, rivers, gurgling creeks, oceans, lakes, artesians. I want to live, sleep, die, within earshot of water.

I fly to Belize for my first SCUBA dive since the procedure. Dive boats are generally pretty personal, you see lots of skin and people changing clothes and stripping off wet for dry. My dive buddy is the only person who knows what I have done, and she is wonderful.

Would you know if you didn't know? I ask her, to reinforce my confidence, to hear the answer again. No, she says. You look great. I stretch out on the lounge chair in the bright Caribbean sunshine. Ironic, I say, telling her about this book, that now I want people to know. We laugh.

I want to tell people what it's really like, I explain to her, help people with the decision. It's not for everyone. I know, she tells me, I know.

While I was there I met the most amazing father-daughter team. He has certified himself and his teenage daughter so that they have something in common that they love to do. I have rarely seen such a relationship and admired it from the first day I met them on the dock.

The final morning of our trip they drove to the poorest section of the city and gave away everything they could think of, extra groceries, soaps gathered from the hotel, bottled water. They gave back.

While we waited for separate planes to take us home to separate places, I told her that if I had a daughter I would wish for one very much like her. Her father is to be admired for raising such an interesting, intelligent person on his own. I hope I see them again someday, and told them so.

Say what needs to be said.

NOVEMBER 7

Eight months to the day after we walked into that Surgical Waiting Room, I do not remember exactly what the Original Girls felt like. Or exactly how they looked.   Or how they moved.   It doesn't matter, because they are gone. This is the new normal. I made the right choice for me, I feel like me.

I spend time with my Dad, bond with my Stepmother, drink coffee and contemplate life with my brother. Drink wine with my Friend Basket.   Buy tickets for next summer's concerts in Saratoga.   I breathe, I enjoy. I go through life with eyes wide open, glass half full.

UNEXPECTEDLY BACK TO MAY 4th...

I have another story about connecting on a plane that I have to add! It is early on a Thursday morning I am going through TSA, flying home after the conference. Remember this is right around the time I was experiencing all those complications with the surgery.

The TSA woman is extremely well-trained, detail oriented, and well, fierce. She is barking orders randomly, loudly, about the rules that we already know. As I pull my second boot off I laugh at something she says, it's just too much! I did not sign up for basic training! Anyway, when I glanced back at the few other folks in line my eyes met with a tall dark haired gentleman who shared my humor at the situation. We smiled. We laughed.

As instructed, I pull out my very dangerous hair gel, toothpaste and conditioner to x-ray them separately, quart Ziploc bag. My carry-on gets pulled out for further inspection by another gloved government agent. Unbeknownst to me now food is a danger! Food. OK, so I always travel with a bag of almonds and peanut butter pretzels, my comfort snack that quells the aforementioned affinity for motion sickness and alleviates the need to pay airport prices. I laugh even harder as she holds them up for all to see, asking what they are. We have created a paranoid society, indeed.

After a thorough inspection the drill sergeant hands me back my breakfast, I gather my wardrobe and am on my way. Tall and handsome is there, at the same gate, heading to Chicago. We exchange another smile.

He is in first class when I board and proceed back to the economy section. Did they take your peanuts? he inquires with an amazing grin and indiscernible accent. You don't have to bring your own, seated up here, I say with a laugh, they'll give you as many as you want.

When I arrive in Chicago he is standing in the terminal and I want to think he is waiting for me. Was he? Yes. We strike up a standard conversation about where we're going and why; I start walking toward my next gate and he joins me. He is from Iceland, of all places. I have been there and he is surprised. I want to go back and SCUBA dive the joining of the tectonic plates, I tell him.

He asks my profession and I explain that I'm a Chef, looking for my next niche, long story... I need a Chef! He replies with enthusiasm. You do? I laugh, that is quite a coincidence! He is serious, and hands me a simple, interesting business card in black and white. Thor. The God of Thunder. What interesting parent names their child after the God of Thunder? I think to myself. Tiny butterflies, this time the good kind, are fluttering. We part, I am smiling.

After his meeting that same evening he calls me! I am stunned to see the ID on my phone. It is late, he is in a taxi cab to his hotel. I am going to see you again, I've already decided, he tells me. He has had a glass or two of wine, and is forthcoming, direct, as most Americans are not. Honest, open, no beating around the bush.

Well, we'll see, I laugh, skeptical, shaking my head at my phone, wondering at the timing of this. I am halfway through the surgeries; I stood before him in Chicago with expanders and silicone scar tape on, those tiny stiches still protruding. I guess that answers the 'You wouldn't know if you didn't know' question well enough! I am thrilled, flattered, disbelieving. I have butterflies.

The geography is challenging, he divided between Texas and Iceland, me in Upstate New York. He looks on a map to see where that is, one night on the phone. Wow, he says, that's way up there! I laugh, oh yes, I tell him, it is.

We stay in touch randomly over the next months, talk on the phone, get to know each other. When I travel and go through TSA I think of him and touch bases, he does the same, most recently in October. He called, we talked. I owe you dinner, he told me. That would be great, I say, because it would. He's quite fascinating, actually, with ideas, energy, and that direct manner of speaking.

NOVEMBER 15

This morning the Icelandic gentleman invited me to an East Coast city to share a bottle of wine. And a couple of days. What do we do, reserve two rooms in the same hotel with one of those adjoining doors? he asks, further charming me as if that was necessary. Sounds like a plan, I tell him, laughing, sounds like a great plan.

Such a rendezvous could certainly mean, gulp, he'll see The New Girls. Up close and personal. Touch them perhaps (yikes!?). My mouth is dry at the prospect. The butterflies awaken, the good ones. I breathe deeply, grab a glass of red wine and search for a flight.

I wasn't perfect before and I'm not perfect now. Cheers to The New Girls.

*If you know someone who needs this book
as a resource and does not have access to it or
needs
guidance at this difficult time,
please contact me.*

Thank you for reading *The New Girls*.

Thank you for sharing my story.

J

Janice Anne Wheeler
SpicingUpTheWorld@gmail.com

9 781795 423496